To

Barbara Nancy Caywood

two top athletes

and fine gals !

Best Wishes

Phil Galvano

GOLF
INSTRUCTION

GOLF INSTRUCTION

BY PHIL GALVANO

PHOTOGRAPHS BY PAUL WING STUDIOS

PUTTER DESIGNED BY PHIL GALVANO

Steffen Publishing Co.,
Holland Patent, N.Y.

To the people
who have made this book possible:

My pupils

– CONTENTS –

BOOK I
SECRETS OF THE PERFECT GOLF SWING

BOOK II
SECRETS OF ACCURATE PUTTING & CHIPPING

– CONTENTS –

BOOK III
THE FINESSE SHOTS OF GOLF

A SUGGESTION –

BEFORE YOU START READING

Don't try to remember everything that is discussed in this book as you read it. Just read casually, as though it were a story. You will be amazed at how much you will effortlessly retain of what you read.

Keep a pencil handy so that you can underline passages that ring a bell with you as you go along. Then, you can refer to them at some later date.

PREFACE

*Practice without science
or a system, is like a pilot
on a ship without a compass.
He knows not where he is going.*
Leonardo Da Vinci

A life time of studying and teaching have enabled me to develop a system for learning the perfect golf swing which is readily adaptable to everyone, regardless of age or physical characteristics.

I want the reader to understand, though, that I have not originated these techniques nor have I created anything new in golf. I have merely evolved a systematic pattern out of the thoughts and experiences of the greatest players. Actually, no one alive today has contributed anything basically new to the playing or teaching of golf. We must all imitate to a certain extent.

Is there any method of teaching golf which is completely correct? Better still, let me ask this question: Are there any professionals teaching today who are teaching incorrectly? No, there are none. Let me give you this illustration. One instructor will say, "Let the hips dominate in the golf swing." He then steps up and drives the ball far and straight down the middle. Another professional will say, "It's not your hips, it's your hands that do the work." He then steps up and hits the ball as far and as straight as the other instructor. A third will say, "It's not your hands, it's your arms that are important." And he, too, will perform equally as well as the others.

Obviously, all three instructors are correct. Why, then, doesn't the pupil show more rapid improvement? The trouble is that he is being taught *incompletely* rather than *incorrectly*.

The golf swing is like a chain with twelve links, each link representing a section of the swing. Each link has value, but unless you have the complete chain, you have nothing.

Let us look at this relationship in another way. Many years before the musical scale was conceived, each teacher of music would claim certain sounds were correct and their pupils were taught by these sounds. A professor of music appeared on the scene, by the name of Guido of Arezza, who remarked, "Why should there be such disagreement? Why not combine the sounds into a basic scale and all work from that scale?" Thus the Guido scale of music was born: Do, re, mi, fa, so, la, ti, do. According to his own statement, a pupil might learn within hours what formerly would have taken him years. Thus, it was for the first time in the history of music that the scale of music, plus the lines of the staff and intervals between them, were systematically used.

This is what I have accomplished in the teaching of golf. I have created a system wherein a pupil will learn in a few months what heretofore took many years to accomplish. You are certain to improve if you have a plan from which to work. With this system of guidance, there is no question that you can reach and perform at your physical peak.

Phil Galvano

BOOK I

SECRETS OF THE PERFECT GOLF SWING

1.
The art of
acquiring skill

BEFORE WE DELVE INTO THE MECHANICS OF THE swing, I should like to explain the necessary steps involved in transforming a physical act from unskilled to supremely skilled.*

A skilled physical act is a movement done with a minimum of conscious thought. In walking, dancing or playing golf, the more we think about the movements involved, the less the skill. No matter how unathletic we are, there are dozens of actions we perform daily that require physical skill. Consequently, our muscles are coordinated through practice until these skills become automatic reactions. If we were to think where to place our feet for each step, we could never walk or dance smoothly or gracefully. If a piano virtuoso had to concentrate on placing his fingers on each key to play a note, or a golfer on the precise movements of his swing, he would be unable to perform with the great speed and smoothness of a topnotch performer.

In true physical skill the muscles of the body respond to the subconscious commands from the brain. If we sud-

---

* The larger part of this chapter also appears in my previous book, *Secrets of Accurate Putting and Chipping.* It is reprinted here because a true understanding of this learning process is essential to improvement in golf.

denly become conscious of our movements, we cannot perform naturally. If we were to concentrate on breathing, we would be exhausted in a very short time. (Try to breath naturally. You will find it impossible unless you stop thinking of it.)

To train ourselves to achieve the highest degree of physical skill in the shortest possible time, we must better understand what takes place in the process of learning. Anyone can improve his skill considerably by becoming aware of the human learning process and by knowing how to make this knowledge work for him.

In learning the starting point is called the normal level. Initially, a rapid climb occurs in the learning curve. This is perfectly logical, for anyone who attempts something for the first time will become more skillful after a period of practice. His progress will be rapid, and the learning curve will rise swiftly.

Somewhere along the learning curve the student begins to progress more slowly and, finally, advancement comes to a temporary standstill. This temporary leveling-off, which psychologists call the "learning plateau," is the point at which our minds analyze the movements involved in an effort to develop even greater skill. In many instances these plateaus may be of extended duration. In some cases we may even drop below the point at which we started, thereby feeling that we have lost our previously developed skill. This is perfectly normal. By continued application, we can again begin a rapid climb in the learning curve. Since each person has a different personality and varying degree of reflexes, he will find that his decline will vary from that of the next person. Before we are able to master a particular skill, we may have a number of these setbacks.

Can we eliminate these declines in the learning curve? Not completely. We can, however, minimize the number of falls and shorten their duration by following these simple rules:

(1) Present the mind with a complete thorough understanding of what is to be done,

(2) Train the body to perform consciously the act that the mind understands, and then,

(3) Perform the act with the ultimate objective in mind.

A person is still relatively unskilled if he performs consciously. However, when he succeeds in mentally putting aside everything he has learned and begins to perform subconsciously—his attention no longer centered on the particular movements involved—then, and only then, will he perform with utmost skill.

As has been stated previously, fluctuations in the learning curve are due to the variety of responses to certain stimulations. These stimulations create movement. The time it takes for these stimulations to create movement is known as "reaction time." Let me illustrate this more concretely. Suppose you are seated in front of a board which has a red light on it, and there are buttons directly in front of you. Your task is to press a button as soon as the red light flashes on. The well-coordinated person will react very quickly to the stimulation of the red light; the less coordinated person will require more time to perform the act. This is called "muscular stimulus" or "length of reaction time."

The same thing occurs in driving. An automobile pulls out of a concealed road onto the main highway in front of you. The well-coordinated driver is able to stop his car in time, or swerve out of danger onto the shoulder of the road or into another lane. The less coordinated person will usually react more slowly, increasing thereby the possibility of a collision. However, do not fear that you may not be gifted with the necessary speed of coordination to avoid danger. Coordination speeds up greatly by itself, simply by continual practice. With the proper guidance, proper coordination can be accomplished in a short time.

The human nervous system, through which reactions are transmitted, is similar to an electrical system. The auto pulls out on the road; our eyes perceive it; and a current is transmitted to the brain, warning of the danger. The brain's alarm system sends signals down to the arms and legs to react by either pressing the foot on the brake or turning the wheel to avoid the trouble. The mere fact that some movement does take place, no matter how slowly, proves that a reaction occurs. Some people react quickly, others more slowly. This difference is due to the length of time it takes for the brain, upon receiving a message, to send a nerve impulse to the particular muscle to be used.

Great physical skill depends on a faster reaction time. However, by repeated practice, the person with the slower reaction time can eventually equal and sometimes exceed the speed of the so-called gifted performer.

Our task, then, is to speed up the impulse of the required action until conscious effort is eliminated, and subconscious, automatic response is developed.

Remember the reaction time test with the button and the light you were asked to imagine before? A series of similar tests have determined that a very fast reaction time is one-fifth of a second. Let's apply this to the swinging of a golf club and assume that you have the fast reaction time of one-fifth of a second. Here is where the difficulties of golf instruction present themselves.

One instructor will say, "Keep your left arm straight." It takes one-fifth of a second for the brain to check if it is straight. Another instructor will say, "Keep your head down." Another fifth is used. Still another will say, "Shift your weight to the right foot on the backswing." That also takes a fifth of a second. So does "Shift to the left on the downswing." Last week you hit a good shot by remembering to keep the right elbow close. One more fifth. You read a book that gave you another suggestion. Again, one-fifth of a second.

The art of acquiring skill

It takes approximately two-fifths of a second to deliver a club head from the top of the backswing to the ball. Therefore, if you think of more than two sections of the swing at the same time, you are exceeding the time required to perform skillfully. The result? Not as good as it should be.

There is only one way of permanently overcoming this obstacle: first, understand completely and thoroughly the actions that must be performed; then, perform these actions consciously, remembering that while you are performing in this manner you will show very little skill. You must continue practicing until the act can eventually be performed without such thorough concentration. In that way you can eventually eliminate the unnecessary fifths of a second that are detrimental to real skill.

The suggestions offered in this book are devised with these proven theories in mind. The finest performers, in all fields of physical dexterity, have gone through these learning stages. Some were aware, and some were not, that these steps were taking place.

By learning the correct movements of your golf swing faithfully, with a conscious realization of what they accomplish, and by continuing to practice diligently until the movements are no longer conscious, you can develop amazing power and accuracy.

There will be many declines in your learning curve. Accept these lapses, for it is through repeated experience that the subconscious truly takes over. Then you will enjoy the pleasure and thrill that accompany true physical accomplishment.

2.
Choosing
your driver

WHAT IS THE OBJECT IN A GAME OF GOLF? TO
propel a golf ball from a given point into a hole some distance away in the fewest number of strokes. In order to
do this, we must learn to hit the ball as far as we can and
as straight as we can.

How is this done? First, we must select the proper driver.
Should it be light or heavy? Let's find out.

If we were to drop two objects of different weights
from the same height, which of the two objects would
land first, the lighter or the heavier object? Try the little
experiment yourself, using an ordinary pencil and your
golf club, or any two objects of noticeably different
weights. Drop both objects from the same height and
notice which of the two lands first. You are now creating
the same experiment that Galileo pèrformed when he
established the principle that bodies of different weights
fall with equal velocities. It proves that the gravitational
pull of the earth is equal with all weights of similar shape.
Both weights land at the same time.

It is a known fact that two objects of different weights
and of similar shape, so as not to create different wind
resistance, when dropped from the same height travel at
the same rate of speed and land at the same time.

Man has not yet found the answer to this mysterious phenomenon. There are many theories about it, but nothing has been proved. All we know is that the pull of the earth is caused by gravity. A great deal, however, is known of the result of this gravitational pull. A falling object increases in speed as it falls and that increase is 32 feet per second, each second. After the first second, the speed of a dropping object is 32 feet per second. At the end of two seconds the falling object is traveling at a speed of 64 feet per second, and so forth. Upon landing the heavier object will have a greater impact force than the lighter object. So, weight plus speed equals force.

In driving a ball any great distance it is not only the impact force that drives the ball a long way; the increasing speed through the ball gives the ball its capacity for great length.

In swinging a golf club it is not the gravitational pull of the earth that pulls the clubhead to the ball. We deliver and generate the clubhead speed with the energy that we ourselves create. I repeat—*we deliver and generate the clubhead speed with the energy that we ourselves create.*

A golf ball is driven a greater distance when *speed* of clubhead, and not weight, is the dominating factor. A club

Choosing your drive

weighing 24 ounces would give very little distance for it could not be swung quickly, whereas a 13-ounce club will give much greater length because of the greater speed that can be generated. The rate of speed of the lighter club creates enough energy to far surpass the impact force of the heavier club. Speed of clubhead is the all-important factor in acquiring great length.

A lighter club can be swung much faster than a heavy club. It is the continued speed of the clubhead through the ball that gives us the long drive, just as it is the tremendous speed of the tiny bullet that gives it its great penetration.

So, in selecting your driver, choose one *that feels light to you,* as each person has a different interpretation of light and heavy.

3.

The flight
of the ball

STILL ANOTHER ELEMENT ENTERS INTO THE PIC-ture—aerodynamics—the effect air resistance has on a moving body.

We all know of the great strength that has been demonstrated by the force of wind. The modern airliner is greatly affected by wind resistance; in fact, it is the very air itself that helps hold up the airliner. Think, then, of how much air friction will influence the flight of the tiny golf ball.

But air resistance can be used as a helpful influence rather than something to be fought, just as the airliner, in battling the air to generate speed, must also depend on the molecules of air itself to keep it aloft. What is the effect air resistance has on a golf ball in motion? In order to answer this question more thoroughly we must first understand what causes a golf ball to travel a great distance in a straight line of flight.

If we place a golf ball on the ground and, using a putter, want to send this ball straight along an imaginary 3 foot line, common sense tells us that the clubface should strike the ball at perfect right angles to the intended line of flight. When this is done, the ball will travel straight along the line, but with overspin. The cause of this overspin is the gravitational pull of the earth on the ball which keeps the ball hugging the ground, thereby creating enough friction to cause the top to keep tumbling over.

When you hear someone saying that now he is able to cause overspin on the ball while putting, you will know that it actually is impossible for a rolling ball in contact with the ground *not* to have overspin. Sidespin may be added to the ball by cutting across in the putting stroke, but there will always be some degree of overspin.

Notice that a golf ball has little grooves or dimples. They were put there for a reason. Many years ago golfers were using balls that had an insufficient amount of grooves. When the balls became old and cut, the players found that these balls, cut or bruised as they were, were traveling truer. Finally they realized that it was the grooves or indentations on the ball that kept it on a straight course. In the air the grooves and indentations on the ball create a

The flight of the ball

vacuum, which in turn causes friction. This friction causes the ball to spin or revolve, thereby giving it a true trajectory.

Have you ever looked into the barrel of a rifle? The barrel is grooved so that the bullet will spin as it leaves the rifle, thereby giving it true flight. That is why the stitches on a baseball are protruding. It is these stitches which continue the spin created by the pitcher, and which cause the ball to travel along a desired line. A tennis player controls the spin of a tennis ball with his racquet because of the fuzz on the ball.

Any sphere traveling in the air will not travel on a true trajectory unless it is revolving. It is the gravitational pull of other planets in the solar system on the mountains and valleys of our earth that keep it rotating. This rotation creates the centrifugal force that keeps the earth in a true orbit.

A glancing blow on a golf ball will cause it to slice or hook. The degree of slice or hook depends upon the sharpness of the angle that the clubface cuts across the intended line of flight. The grooves on a golf ball keep it traveling in the direction of the spin. You probably have noticed that while on the driving range the ball sometimes takes crazy dives. If you were to check the ball before hitting it, you would find that with all the hitting it has received, the grooves on the ball have been worn smooth, thereby creating no spinning action on the ball. Some golfers feel that it is their golf swings that are at fault, but in this case, the condition of the golf ball is responsible for the poor shot. Always check the balls you are using to make sure they are in good condition.

If, when the clubface strikes the ball, an insufficient amount of force is delivered to the ball, it will not take off or become airborne—it will roll end over end. But when enough force is delivered, the reaction on the ball is entirely different. The ball depresses against the clubface and, for an instant, the clubhead and ball travel at the same rate of speed. Then the elasticity of the ball causes the ball to expand, thereby giving it a forward thrust.

The forward thrust is so great that the ball, in its early flight, has little or no spin. As the force diminishes the ball begins to acquire an underspin, making it rise sharply and then dropping very quickly and stopping. Stroking the ball straight along the intended line of flight will give a degree of accuracy but not greatest length. In order to get maximum length we must create the proper spinning action on the ball which, in turn, will enable the ball to run those extra precious yards after it lands.

You have probably experienced hitting a drive with a great flight, and then having the fellow you are playing with hit a low grounder that keeps running and running until his drive is as far out as your clean hit. The spin on the ball is responsible.

The flight of the ball

If the clubface strikes the ball with the clubhead travel-ing across the intended line of flight, from right to left, the ball will travel straight until the major part of the forward thrust is spent, and then curve to the right. This is your well-known "slice." It is undesirable, when great distance is required, for the ball has a tendency to stop when it comes in contact with the ground. Another rea-son why an outside in path with the clubhead will not give you great length is that, in an outside in stroke, the arms are pulling in across the intended line of flight and only the force created by the arm action is delivered to the ball. The great power of the large muscles of your body are not utilized.

This does not mean that good golf cannot be played with the ball curving toward the right. Good golf *can* be played with the ball slicing or curving to the right. All you have to do is allow for the curve of the ball, but the greater the length, the easier the second shot.

If a ball is struck with the clubface traveling from the inside to the outside of the line of flight—that is from close to your body across the intended line of flight and away from you—first, the tremendous force of your entire body is directed behind the blow delivered to the ball; second, an amazing reaction takes place upon the ball. The major part of the force is pushing the ball to the right, while the ball spins to the left. This prevents the ball from drifting to the right, thereby keeping the ball on a straight course.

The flight of the ball

These two forces, the thrust to the right and the spin to the left, react upon one another giving the ball a liveliness and lifting quality that is almost magical. This results in a continuous straight flight with a power that seems to ignore the elements.

So, for accuracy and length, the first and one of the most important rules of good golf is that your clubhead, with the clubface at a perfect right angle to the intended line of flight, must travel from the inside to the outside of the intended line of flight. This will result in a straight, long flight.

As long as the clubface, traveling in the proper in-to-out path, strikes the ball at a perfect right angle to the intended line of flight, the ball will travel a straight line. If the angle at which you cut across the line of flight from the outside is too sharp, you will have a hook. The angle of the in-to-out swing must be very slight in the hitting area. (The hitting area is 6 inches in front of the ball to 6 inches in back of the ball.) The clubface must enter the hitting area from the inside of the intended line of flight to the outside, at an angle of not more than *half the diameter of the ball.*

This is the most important part of your swing insofar as accuracy is concerned. You may have a fine looking golf swing but if there is poor contact between the club-face and ball, your ball will never travel straight. You can have perfect contact between clubface and ball and a

A. Ball struck with outside-in stroke will cause a slice.

B. Ball struck with a too sharp in-to-out path will cause a hook.

C. Ball struck with club head traveling at very slight in-to-out path will result in a perfect flight.

very poor looking swing, and still get the ball to go out perfectly straight. That is the reason you sometimes see golfers with strange looking swings playing fairly good golf. All they are doing is contacting the ball at a perfect right angle with the clubface traveling along the correct in-to-out path.

A golf ball can be missed with a perfect grip. It can be missed keeping the head still. It can be missed with a perfectly straight left arm, with perfect balance, perfect foot work, hitting against the left side, and all the other must that have been presented to the struggling golfer.

A ball can be driven straight with a bad grip, with the head moving, with the left arm bent; it can be driven straight with any poor or unconventional form. As long as you have perfect contact between clubface and ball, the ball will travel straight.

A swing that is perfect merely means that the maximum clubhead speed is being generated at the moment of impact. The more perfect the swing, the greater the clubhead speed. The result is a longer drive. It has nothing to do with accuracy. Accuracy comes only through perfect contact between clubface and ball.

Now that we have a better understanding of what makes a golf ball travel in a straight line, let's consider the next most essential requirement for good golf—*length.*

The flight of the ball

Without length it is impossible to play par golf with any consistency. One of the reasons the modern golfer is able to score so well is because of the tremendous length he gets off the tee. You can hit the ball as straight as possible, but if you can't reach the green with your next shot on the long par four holes, it's going to be difficult to get your pars and almost impossible to get any birdies. In order to get great length we must be able to generate the greatest clubhead speed upon contact of clubface and ball. *This is where form enters into the picture—the more perfect the form, the longer the drive.* Length without accuracy is of little value, and so is accuracy without length.

To summarize, there are two basic requirements for good golf:

(1) *Accuracy*
For accuracy, you must hit the ball with the clubhead traveling from the inside of the intended line of flight to the outside of the intended line of flight.

(2) *Length*
For length, you must generate the maximum clubhead speed at contact point of clubface and ball.

The flight of the ball

Before we begin our discussion of the technique of form which results in generating maximum clubhead speed, let me ask you this question: "Are you satisfied with the way you are hitting the ball?" If you are, then no one can say you are swinging incorrectly. But let me ask one more question: "Are you getting the most out of your physical equipment?" If you are not, then this book was written for you.

4.

Body Alignments

Position Number 1

THE PERFECT GOLF SWING GENERATES THE MAXI-mum *clubhead* speed upon contact with the ball as the clubhead is traveling in the proper path. Let's assume that a perfect golf swing is able to generate a force in which maximum is equivalent to 100 per cent. You do not need a 100 per cent force swing to play great golf. You can play great golf with a 90 per cent, or even 80 per cent, force swing. The closer to a 100 per cent your swing is, the further the ball will go. Many of our good players of today do not have 100 per cent swings, but this doesn't mean that they aren't playing good golf. It means, though, that they are not getting the full power they are capable of generating.

That is why, at times, a little fellow will outdrive a much bigger man. The more perfect the swing, the greater the power. The tall person, although he may not have a perfect swing, is creating such a large arc (a greater circle gives greater speed), that he is generating enough force to send the ball out far enough to be able to reach the green with his second shot. The small man must have a near perfect swing; otherwise, he could not develop enough to score. By the same token, a woman, in order to play well, usually needs a more perfect swing than does a man because of her physical limitations.

In building a perfect golf swing it is not necessary to tear down the swing you have—you merely add to your swing.

Let's suppose that a perfect golf swing is like a chain with 12 links and each section of the swing is represented by a link. If any of the links are missing you are not going to perform up to par. You many have five, six, or even seven links in your golf swing but that is not quite enough, so you merely add until you have all the links necessary to complete the chain of a perfect golf swing. The more links you have, the greater the degree of clubhead speed.

Do not feel that it is impossible for you to have a perfect swing, for, if presented properly, it becomes a very simple procedure to acquire one. Actually, the perfect swing comes by trial and error if you devote enough time to practice and playing. This way of developing the perfect swing would take approximately fifteen years of devotion and hard work. But with the proper guidance, *it can also be done in a matter of hours.*

The first step in building the super swing is to check and correct your "address position." This, I believe, is the most important link in your whole golf chain, without which it is practically impossible to score consistently well. It's like shooting the world's most expensive rifle— if you do not aim accurately you will not hit your target.

The correct "address position" will give you a sound foundation upon which to build your super golf swing. This foundation will apply to everyone regardless of height, size, shape or age.

In building your perfect address position let's ignore the surface muscles and go to the bones of your body, for if you are skeletally correct, only then can you be muscularly perfect.

Position Number One

We know that two essentials of a good golf swing are clubhead speed and the proper clubpath. Notice that I list clubhead speed ahead of proper clubpath. Actually, maxi-

Body alignment: Position number 1

mum clubhead speed, with the correct body alignment, will cause the clubhead to travel along the proper path.

The first requisite in generating maximum clubhead speed is the creating of the largest possible arc, for greater speed is dependent on a greater swinging circle. There are certain skeletal positions that enable one, with just a minimum of effort, to create the greatest arc and cause the clubhead to travel along the desired path at tremendous speed.

As I said before, these skeletal positions can be learned by trial and error after many years of experimentation. Some people are gifted with the correct positions from the start, others are not so fortunate. To make sure you are skeletally correct, let's start right at the bottom with the position of the feet.

Stand with your heels on an imaginary straight line parallel with the intended line of flight. The center of your heels should be spread apart to a width equivalent to that of your hips. If a person with narrow shoulders and wide hips sets his feet as far apart as the width of his shoulders, he would find it difficult to create the firm foundation necessary for a proper swing.

If your feet are too close together, you are going to have too much turn. If they are too far apart, too little turn. Your feet should be far enough apart so as to give you enough body balance to resist the tremendous force that will be generated by the clubhead speed. Another way of finding this correct stance is to imagine that you are

Body alignment: Position number 1

going to catch a bag of sand being dropped from above. If your feet were too close together you would not be able to catch too great a weight; if too far apart, you would collapse under the weight. Set your feet far enough apart so as to give you a solid foundation with perfect balance. In doing this you will find that the heels of your feet will wind up, approximately, a distance apart equal to the width of your hips.

If both your feet are placed straight at a right angle to the imaginary line the bone structure of your ankles will confine your ability to turn. The toes and heels are a tremendous factor in governing the length of the backswing and the length of the follow-through. Both toes should be equally turned out approximately 3 inches from the straight position. You may find it difficult to judge 3 inches exactly. If you are a little off one way or the other, don't worry about it.

Turning out your toes gives your ankles greater freedom and makes your turn easier. It will also give you an equal pivot release both ways. Try swinging with both toes pointed straight out and, unless you are double-jointed, you will find that both the backswing and the follow-through are restricted. Pointing your toes out too much will also restrict the swing. Make sure that your toes are pointed out as close to the 3 inch mark as possible.

The weight of your body must be balanced between the balls of your feet and your heels, with a preponderance of weight toward your heels. The position of your feet plus the correct weight distribution will give you a foundation solid enough to eventually resist, with perfect balance, any amount of centrifugal force you will generate.

Now that you have the correct position of the feet and the proper weight distribution, let us continue upward to the knees.

Your knees should be unlocked to the extent that your height will not be affected. Your legs will thus remain springy and flexible, with a minimum of strain in your thighs and calves. Bending the knees too much creates tension in your thighs, causing you to be too conscious of the degree of bend your knees must maintain during the swing.

With your knees in the unlocked position, stand as tall as you possibly can. Feel as if you are lifting both hips up as high as you can without straightening your knees, and learn to keep your hips at this high level. You will eventually understand the importance of this.

Now, relax your arms until they are hanging by your sides as limply as two lengths of rope. If you have trouble relaxing your arms, lift them over your head and then let them drop to your sides. With your arms relaxed, bend forward slightly from the waist up by pushing your buttocks just a little further back than the line of your heels. You should bend forward from the waist up until your relaxed arms and fingertips are pointing straight down in

Body standing up straight in preparation for the correct address position, feet proper distance apart, center of heels in line with hips. Toes turned out to enable full free turn in both directions. Weight slightly back on heels. Knees unlocked to extent it does not affect height.

The Ape Position (front view). Arms hanging down limply. Body bent at waist so that hands and arms are hanging down, relaxed in line with toes.

The Ape Position (side view). Body bent slightly from waist, arms hanging down relaxed like ropes. Hands in line with toes.

The Ape Position (three-quarter view). Head is held up high.
Eyes are peering down at ball.

Body alignment: Position number 1

a line with your toes. In bending forward slightly, do not bow the head. Keep it up as it was when standing straight.

Your arms and hands are now at the proper distance from your body. Your body is now set in the correct basic position, a foundation strong enough to house the ideal golf swing.

This body set is a position of tremendous power. The body is relaxed and yet ready to move in any direction. This is the on-guard-and-alert position of the strongest two-legged mammal in the world—the ape. It is called the "ape stance," and in golf it is the most essential position for great power.

Check the ape stance carefully, then step away and resume the same position again. Do it a few times. Get yourself familiar with the ape stance for, with the exception of your arms and hands, it is the eventual position your body will assume when you are in perfect alignment. This body set from the waist up is the essential foundation for the correct address position. Step away and again resume the ape stance, this time holding your driver in your left hand. Remember that in the ape stance both arms and hands are hanging as limply as ropes. While in this relaxed position, you will notice that your hands are hanging down approximately in front of your thighs.

The club should be placed in the left hand while the left hand is in the hanging down position. The left hand and arm must remain at its same angle. There must be

Body alignment: Position number 1

no pronation or turning of the left hand in either direction.

With the left hand still holding the club and the club resting in its natural position, you will find that the left hand will be slightly ahead of the clubface. The left hand which holds the clubhandle will be approximately in front of your left thigh. For each person the position of the left hand in relation to the left thigh will be different, depending upon the size, shape, and the formation of the individual's shoulders. The object is to determine where the position of the left hand is in relation to your type of build, and train yourself to address the ball with your left hand as close to this position as possible. In this way, full power and consistency can be developed.

While you are still holding the club in the left hand, relax the left hand so that you will be holding the club lightly enough to allow the clubhead to rest, of its own weight, on the ground. The spot where the sole of the clubface touches the ground is the bottom or the lowest point in your arc, and it is also known as the center point of your arc. This center point is the spot where you should tee up your ball for your particular type of build. Check this center point in the arc in relation to your left heel so that, in this way, you will have a constant reminder.

Pay particular attention to the location of the exact spot of the center point in your arc, as this point may vary slightly to the left or to the right, depending upon the build of the individual. This center point, the bottom of

Ape Position with club in left hand. Note left arm and hand at same position in relation to left thigh. As in the Ape Position clubhead ends up in its proper place. Shoulders are at an equal height.

Body alignment: Position number 1

the arc, is where the clubhead stops descending and starts
to rise.

The position of the body from the waist up, by the
lowering and raising of your trunk, will regulate the depth
of the center point. Raise your body from the waist up by
standing taller, and you will notice that the left arm, while
still extended and holding the club, will also rise as a result of the raising of the back. This, in turn, will lift the
clubhead from the ground. The lifting of the clubhead
should not be done with the left arm but by the raising of
the back. The taller you stand, the farther away from the
ground will the clubhead be. In gauging the correct depth
you should first raise and then lower the clubhead by raising and lowering your back until the clubhead rests
lightly on the ground. This raising and lowering of your
back will be your gauge for the correct alignment insofar
as depth is concerned. The bending of your left arm will
destroy the depth gauge, so keep the left arm relaxed
enough to enable the weight of the club to keep your arm
extended, so that you get the feeling that the weight of the
club is stretching the arm.

This depth of the arc is measured by the distance from
the front of the throat (the point more commonly known
as the Adam's apple) to the ball. After setting yourself
correctly, keep the distance from the Adam's apple to the
ball the same until after the ball is struck (no gulping,
please). If you widen this distance before the ball is hit

Body alignment: Position number 1

by the straightening of the left arm, you will have a tendency toward topping the ball. If you shorten the distance between the Adam's apple and the ball by bowing or by bending the knees too much, there will be a tendency to hit the ground in back of the ball unless you compensate by pulling in your left arm. This is not wise as you will again destroy your gauge, and you will never be able to develop any great degree of consistency of performance.

You have probably seen golfers who bend over so much at the start of their swings that there is not enough room for their arms and the full length of the club shaft to come through to the ball freely. In each swing the arms must make a muscular adjustment in an effort to hit the ball. Otherwise, the ball will not be hit.

This cannot be done with great accuracy because too much attention must be given to the muscles involved. The body is actually fighting itself. You are trying to generate great clubhead speed while, at the same time, you are trying to guide the clubhead to the ball by pulling in your arms.

The less the strength or muscle power used in an act, the easier the repetition of the act.

Adjusting the distance from the Adam's apple to the ball is an act that requires very little attention; in fact, this distance can be maintained while the body is almost completely relaxed. In adjusting this distance, make sure that you have enough room to allow your extended left

Body alignment: Position number 1

arm and the full length of your club shaft to travel freely through to the ball.

After you adjust to the proper depth, maintain the distance from the Adam's apple to the ball until well after the ball is hit. It would not hurt to check this point from time to time, especially when faced with the problem of a difficult shot. More balls are missed because of improper depth than for any other reason. After practicing this simple depth adjustment, you will find that in a little while you will not have to give it too much attention, as your body will instinctively adjust itself with amazing ease.

To prove this, try this little experiment. All you have to do is look at a clock. Choose a large clock not too far away from you. Now look at the clock focusing your eyes on the number two. Then after you have focused your eyes on the number two, look away from the clock for an instant. Then, look back at the clock, and you will find that your eyes will instinctively focus again on the number two. A *nerve pattern,* once formed (unless forced otherwise), will repeat itself.

Learning this depth adjustment will also be an invaluable aid in playing an explosion shot out of the sand; not only must your feet be dug in below the level of the ball in an effort to lower the bottom of the arc, but your body from the waist up must, also, be bent a little more than usual so as to make sure that the depth of the center point

Body alignment: Position number 1

of the bottom of the arc is underneath the ball. The same applies when you play the ball from a lie where the ball is below the level of your feet, it is not necessary to also bend your knees a greater distance. A little more bowing of your body from the waist up will take care of the necessary adjustment. If the ball happens to lie above the level of your feet, shorten the distance from the Adam's apple to the ball by standing taller.

Under normal conditions, that is with little or no wind, play the ball at the exact center point of the arc. In doing this, make sure that you adjust the depth of the arc so that the clubface picks the ball up as cleanly as possible. This will give you the best type of flight. If you have a bad lie or when the ball is not sitting just right, lower the depth of the arc slightly. If, because of wind conditions, you want the ball to have a high trajectory, play the ball slightly to the left of the center point. If, when playing against the wind, you want a low flight on your ball, play it slightly to the right of the center point. Play the ball where it will give you the type of trajectory you desire.

You may hear someone say, "I cannot take a divot."

Taking a divot is merely the result of playing the ball slightly to the right of the center point. As the clubhead is descending, the clubface meets the ball before the clubface touches the ground and then, after it has hit the ball, it continues downward to take the divot. The ball is actually hit before the clubhead has reached the bottom of its arc.

Body leans over slightly toward right in preparation for placing right hand on club for proper grip. Right hand and right shoulder drop below left shoulder and left hand. Right shoulder remains in back of left shoulder.

Without disturbing position of left hand and left arm, bring right hand over to left and place right hand in proper grip without disturbing the position of the club face. You are now set for maximum power and accuracy. Be sure to keep right shoulder and right arm in back of left shoulder and arm.

Body alignment: Position number 1

For best results play the ball at the center point in the arc. Make sure that you regulate the depth of the arc by keeping the distance from the Adam's apple to the ball the same until well *after* the ball is hit.

Again resume the ape stance holding the club in your left hand. Your right arm and hand should hang down limply in front of your right thigh. Leaving the left hand where it is, tilt the trunk of your body slightly to the right. This tilt of the trunk to the right will lower the right shoulder, right arm, and right hand. The tilt to the right should be very slight, not more than two inches. In tilting to the right, *do not push the right shoulder forward.* Simply lower it. You will note that the left shoulder is now higher than your right shoulder. Leaving the left hand where it is, again making sure *you keep the right arm and right shoulder from pushing forward,* bring the right hand and right arm down, under, and over to the left and place it on the club. Then, without turning the angle of the right hand, overlap the little finger of your right hand over the forefinger of your left hand while still keeping the right arm bent and the right elbow close to your body. The exact position of the grip of the hands on the club at this time is not too important, as I shall later describe the grip in full detail.

You should now be in the correct address position. So, to be sure you are correct, let us check.

The center of the back of your heels should be as far apart as the width of your hips. The weight of your

Position #1. The Correct Address (alignment) Position. Head held high. Look at ball with depth eye. Left shoulder higher than right shoulder. Left arm more extended than right arm. Weight slightly back on heels. Angle of shoulders and arms along the in-to-out path. Knees unlocked to extent height is not affected.

Address Position #1 (side view). Note angle of arms and shoulders.

Body alignment: Position number 1

body should be distributed between the balls of your feet and your heels, with a slight tendency of greater weight toward your heels. Your knees should be bent only to the extent that it does not affect your height. Your body is bent with your head held high enough to give you the impression that you are peering down at the ball. Your left shoulder is higher than your right shoulder. Your left arm is extended and practically resting on top of the left chest pectoral muscle. Your right arm is bent with your right elbow pointing in close to the right side of your body.

Your feet should be aligned so that the back of your heels are parallel to the intended line of flight. This alignment of heels and line of flight should be like railroad tracks—the intended line of flight would be one track and the line of the heels the other track. Your buttocks should also be parallel to the line of your heels and the intended flight line. If a line were drawn across the front of your chest at shoulder height from shoulder to shoulder, this line should be pointing to the right of the intended target. The arms should also be pointing to the right of your intended target and parallel with the line of the shoulders. The line of the shoulders and the line across the arms should be parallel with the inside-out path that the club-head will take.

This is the perfect body alignment for the proper address and we shall call it Position #1, the address. In addressing the ball, great care must be exercised to make sure you are in this proper alignment.

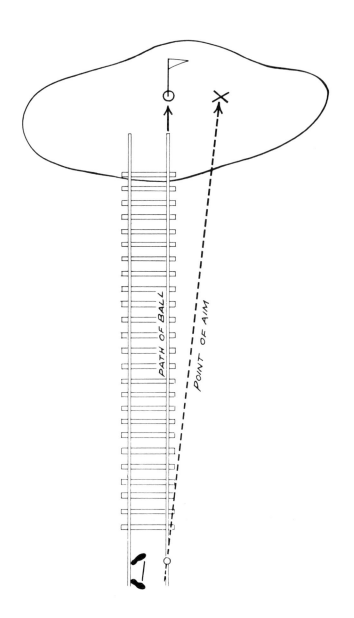

PATH OF BALL

POINT OF AIM

Body alignment: Position number 1

ARROW SHOWS DIRECTION BALL WILL GO

PATH OF CLUB HEAD

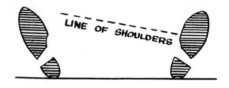

LINE OF SHOULDERS

As in aiming a rifle, if the body is not aligned correctly for the proper address, you will never hit the target. Your heels, buttocks, shoulders, front part of your arms, and the clubface, are the sights in your golf gun. So, before swinging, make sure that each point is aligned accurately.

Position No. 1, the address, may seem uncomfortable in the beginning, but take a look at yourself in a mirror and you will realize that you look much better than you feel. It is a good idea to practice the address position in front of a mirror so that you can see as well as feel the correctness of it. Practice the address position until you can

Body alignment: Position number 1

almost do it automatically. Start with the feet first, then the body-weight, the knees, the trunk, the head, shoulders, arms, and, last of all, a casual attention to your hands.

Incidentally, the basic foundation of this address position will apply for all your full shots from the driver down to your full wedge shot. The length of the club will take care of the necessary changes. As the club gets shorter, so your stance becomes slightly narrower.

Let's examine this address position more closely and find out why it should be set this way.

1. *Why should the left shoulder be higher than the right shoulder?*

If we were to hold the golf club with both hands together on the club, the shoulders would be at an equal height. The right hand is placed below the left hand. This causes you to do either of three things; raise the left shoulder, bend the left arm, or lower the right shoulder. Raising the left shoulder would create tension in that shoulder. This is not good, for the freer you are from tension, the better your swing will be. Bending the left arm at the address would destroy the depth gauge and would result in a faulty alignment; for when the clubhead meets the ball, the force of the clubhead will keep the left arm extended. If it is not at the extended position at the start an adjustment will be necessary as you come into the ball. At times this adjustment will not be exactly correct. So, why add another thought and movement in your swing? The most natural thing to do is to lower the right shoulder for, as you come into the ball, the right shoulder will naturally be lower than the left. This, in turn, will result in the left shoulder being higher.

2. *Why should the head and chin be held up at the address, making one peer down at the ball?*

If the head were held down so that the chin is practically resting on your throat, the bent position of your head, as you took your back-swing, would cause tension at the top of your spine, thereby restricting freedom in your turn. Also, if you took your back-swing with your chin down, your shoulder would be prevented from taking the full turn. The chin should be raised high enough to allow sufficient room for the shoulder to pass under the chin.

3. *Why should the right arm be tucked in at the start?*

If the right arm were straight at the start in the address position, the arm would straighten out, as we came into the ball, causing you to swing across the intended line of flight from the outside in. There are a few good golfers who do start with the right arm straight at the address, but as they swing into the ball they must make the necessary adjustment of coming into the ball with the right arm bent and tucked into the right side. Under emotional pressure you may not remember to tuck the right arm in as you hit the ball. Therefore, it is better to start with the arm bent so that the adjustment will not be necessary.

Body alignment: Position number 1

Most of the top golfers do start with the right arm tucked in.

You are probably wondering why I have not gone into the grip in greater detail. The reason is that you are not quite ready for the perfect grip as yet, for I cannot give you the proper grip until we are sure that your arms are in the correct position. The adjustment of the hands depends on the correct position of the arms. Similarly, I cannot adjust your arms until your shoulders are correct, nor can I set your shoulders right until the trunk, legs, and feet are in the correct position. That is why we began building the swing from the feet up.

It is like a sculptor creating a statue of a golfer. First he must set the armature or wire in the position he wishes the statue to portray. Then he must put clay roughly over the entire frame with enough bulk so that, eventually, detail can be obtained. If he then started to carve out the hands to perfection, he would have to build everything to fit the hands. That would not be wise as he would be building backwards. For example, when Michelangelo painted a woman lying on a couch covered with a wrap he first sketched the skeleton, then painted the flesh on the body, then painted the wrap over the body, thereby creating the great depth and perfection that only he was capable of.

Following the same procedure, working from the skeletal frame out will make it easier to eventually be muscularly correct. When we attain muscular perfection then

Body alignment: Position number 1

you shall be guided in the advanced methods of releasing the subconscious muscular controls until supreme physical skill is attained. At this point in your progress do not strive for exact detail. Get the over-all rough bulk that is essential for ultimate perfection.

Body alignment: Position number 1

SUMMARY

The Golf Sights in Body Alignment

The Address

—Position No. 1

Feet	The center of your heels apart the width of your hips. Line of heels parallel with intended line of flight.
Toes	Both toes out 3 inches.
Weight	Between balls of feet and heels, slightly more toward heels.
Buttocks	Extended just slightly past your heels.
Trunk	Bent over in "ape position" until relaxed. Arms and fingers point to toes.
Shoulders	Left shoulder slightly higher than right shoulder.
Arms	Left arm extended and right arm bent with right elbow close and pointing in toward right hip.

5.
Finish of the swing: Position Number 3

WHILE IN THE ADDRESS POSITION, NOTICE THAT the line of your heels and the intended line of flight are parallel. The intended line of flight will go directly to the target while the line of the heels will end up to the left of the target. One line on target, the other to the left of target.

The ball will travel along the intended line of flight only if you allow the clubhead to swing across the flight line along an in-to-out path; a club path that seems to be directed to the right of your target. Your shoulders and arms should be set parallel to the in-to-out line you expect your clubhead to travel through.

Being aware of the path your clubhead should travel, take a full swing in your own way and make an effort to swing the clubhead along the in-to-out path. Now, again take a swing but this time stay at the finish of your swing for a moment and check the position of your right foot. If your right foot is not turned up and resting on its toe or if the heel is still down at the finish of your swing, you have restricted the follow-through.

If your head is still looking and pointing toward the

spot where the ball was teed-up another restriction is added, and a full follow-through is impossible unless you are double-jointed. In order to have a full follow-through, both the head and the right foot must turn and come up at the finish of your swing. The head does not stay down, nor does the heel of the right foot.

You will probably notice that golfers who do not come up on their right toe will usually have a narrow stance. This is done instinctively. Nature forces you to have a narrow stance so as to protect your spine. Incidentally, by coming up on your right toe you will help prevent any back injury that may result from the unnatural twist that is caused by keeping your right heel down. With a little practice the heel will come up by itself and cause you to finish your swing. Another, and equally important, barometer of the follow-through is your head. If your head is still looking and pointing down at the spot where the ball was resting, the follow-through is almost impossible unless your body is extremely flexible.

The head does not stay down throughout the swing. If you keep your head down you may injure your spine.

Finish of the swing: Position number 3

The great force will come to an abrupt halt by the strain and twisting of the spinal column in the neck area. Second, you *cannot* complete the follow-through that should be allowed to take place. The head must come up after the ball is hit and you must be on the right toe at the finish of the swing so that you are looking straight toward the line of flight.

You may hear some instructors say that the right foot and the head will turn and come up by themselves as a result of the swing. In some cases this is so, but in most cases, *this is not so*. The turning of the body will not turn the head properly nor bring the right foot on its toe unless you, yourself, do it. However, there are some golfers who do have the proper reaction from the start but in most cases you must do it yourself.

To make sure you have a full follow-through, see to it that at the finish of your swing you are on the right toe and that your head is turned and facing the intended target.

You may say, "I am not flexible enough to have a full follow-through."

This is not so. Anyone of any size, shape, or age can have a full follow-through if you come up on your right toe and you are facing the target at the finish of the swing. If done properly there should be little or no twisting of the spinal column. The body should be free from strain. Keeping the head down and not coming up on the right

Finish of the swing: Position number 3

toe will cause a tremendous amount of twisting pressure on your spinal cords and back. In order to relieve this twisting pressure make sure you come up on your right toe and turn your head toward the target.

The next time you play, notice that golfers who do not have a full follow-through will usually have one or both of these faults. They have kept their heads down too long or have not come up on the right toe.

In the perfect follow-through position the head faces the target. The right shoulder is slightly ahead of the left shoulder. The body has little or no tension. The left leg is straight with the majority of weight of the body resting on the left leg. The right leg is relaxed and bent at the knee with the right foot on its toe. We shall call this—Position No. 3—the finish.

The key points of Position No. 3—the finish—are: head facing the target, right shoulder slightly ahead of left shoulder, right leg bent and relaxed, with the right foot resting on its toe.

Practice this follow-through position until you can do it easily. In the beginning, as you practice, you may find yourself losing your balance. If you are losing your balance backward, it means that at the address you started with too much weight resting on your heels. If you lose your balance forward at the finish, it usually means that your weight was too far forward at the address. The direction you lose your balance will indicate where the unbalance

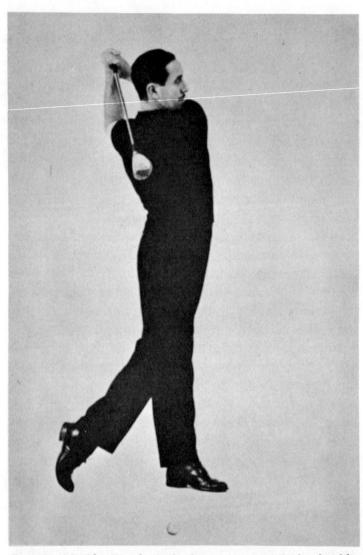

Position #3, The Finish. Right foot on its toe. Right shoulder turned in front of left shoulder. Head looking at target.

Position #3, The Finish. Right foot on its toe. Right shoulder
ahead of left shoulder. Head not down but up and looking
at target.

Finish of the swing: Position number 3

of weight occurred at the start.

Another thing to be aware of in losing your balance is that at the base of our ears we have equilibrium ducts which are circular canals with fluid in them. In the fluid are little hairs. The movement of ·the body causes the fluid to move which, in turn, causes the little hairs to bend in the particular direction of the movement. Upon bending, these little hairs contact the nerve centers in the particular area affected. In turn, the nerve centers indicate the direction of the movement. Until the nerves become acquainted with a new movement you may lose your balance, but by repetition the nerves will soon become accustomed to the new movement and your balance will be perfect.

Let me ask a question pertaining to the follow-through. Is it necessary in a golf swing to have a full follow-through? Why not hit the ball, then stop?

After all it has been proven by photography that after contact between clubface and ball, the golf ball leaves the face of the club before the clubhead has traveled a few inches. So, why must you have a full follow-through when you swing? Why not just hit the ball and then stop?

Here is the reason. When we swing we want the greatest speed at the contact point of clubhead and ball.

The greatest speed in a swinging circle is at the center of its arc. So, if your swing ends just a little past the ball, the center of the arc is backed up accordingly, and your greatest speed will be spent way before you hit the ball. By the time your clubhead reaches the ball, the clubhead has already starfed to slow down. This results in great loss of power and distance.

Let me cite a more visual example. Let us assume you were to drive a golf ball under a plate glass window which is only three feet in front of the ball. The ball will travel under the glass but the clubhead will crash into the pane of glass in the course of its follow-through. Do you think that you can hit that ball very hard and not crash into the pane of glass? No. You would have to start slowing down way before you met the ball in order not to crash into the glass.

If you want to drive a golf ball a long way, then all restrictions must be removed to enable the club to lash through the ball violently until the club comes to its final resting place. So, as stated before, keeping the head down must be eliminated. Also, the right heel must come up so that the swing can have a free and full follow-through.

Practice this follow-through position for without it your greatest length can never be attained.

Without a full follow-through your club would describe only half a circle. By giving you a better Position No. 1—the address—and a better Position No. 3—the finish—you are now creating a full circle. (The top of the back-swing is Position No. 2. We shall discuss this position later on.)

The need for a full, free follow through: If you were asked to drive a golf ball under a pane of glass and not crash into the glass with your clubhead, it would be impossible to hit the ball with too much force, since the momentum would force the clubhead to crash into the glass pane. In preventing the clubhead from crashing into the glass it would be necessary to start slowing up the clubhead long before the ball is reached. If the follow-through is restricted, the clubhead hits the ball as it is slowing up; result, very little distance.

Finish of the swing: Position number 3

By going from Position No. 1—the address—back then to Position No. 3—the finish—you will be creating a full circle. For a while your circle will be very uneven but after you begin to show consistency your circle will begin to become truer and smoother. You will, then, start to show some consistency in your driving.

Try this little experiment. Address the ball properly. Then close your eyes and swing. Go from the start Position No. 1—the address—back and through to Position No. 3—the finish—keeping your eyes closed. You will find that you will still be able to hit the ball. It proves that your body is now set properly for your type of build. (Don't forget to open your eyes after the swing.) The reason you hit the ball with your eyes closed is because you trusted your positions and did not try to guide the clubhead to the ball. Remember this—*trust your swing and it will behave properly. Try to guide the clubhead to the ball, and inaccuracies will enter into your swing.*

Practice in your own way going from Position No. 1—the address—back and then to Position No. 3—the finish. Practice this until you can go from Position No. 1 to Position No. 3 naturally and with little attention. You should now begin to see some improvement in your driving. You should be sending the ball further and beginning to show some consistency. By merely going from Position No. 1—the address—to Position No. 3—the finish—you should attain enough power to enable you to score under 100, providing you have some system of putting and chipping.

STANCE

Square stance ● In this stance, both heels are on a straight line parallel with the intended line of flight.

Closed stance ● In the closed stance, start with the heels on a straight line parallel with the intended line of flight. Then bring the left foot slightly forward.

Open stance ● Start again with the heels on a straight line parallel with the line of flight. Leave the right foot where it is and step back slightly with the left foot.

Finish of the swing: Position number 3

Let me suggest a book on putting and chipping. I forget who the author was but I enjoyed reading it very much and I have to admit that, by using his system, my putting and chipping improved considerably. I think the title is *Secrets of Accurate Putting and Chipping.**

Just going from Position No. 1 to Position No. 3 without analyzing or trying to check and control the swing, you will find that you will start driving straighter and farther with much more consistency and less effort.

Here is a little exercise that you can do at home without a club that will help train you to keep your balance and to follow-through properly.

Stand up straight facing a wall in your room; then place your hands as shown on p. 65. Put your feet as far apart as they were in the address position. Focus your eyes on a spot on the wall. While still looking at this spot, turn your shoulders and hips to the right until you are facing the wall on the right. In turning to the right it is correct to turn your left foot part way so that the left heel rises off the ground.

Pause, and then turn to the left past the wall in front of you until you are facing the wall on the left. As you face this wall you should be on the tip of the right toe and, as in the finish of your swing, your head, shoulders, and entire body face the left wall.

Secrets of Accurate Putting and Chipping by Phil Galvano...see Book II section starting on page 177.

Finish of the swing: Position number 3

Do this exercise twenty times each morning for the first couple of weeks of your learning period and you will be amazed at the balance and the ease with which you will assume Position No. 3.

Exercise for learning the body follow thru. *Position A.* Interlace the middle fingers of your hands. Elbows at shoulder height. Thumbs resting on chest. This exercise can also be done with hands on hips.

Position B. Turn mostly from the waist up. Do not let the elbows or left shoulder dip in the process of turning.

Position C. Finish of exercise. Body facing left. Right foot on its toe. Head looking straight out toward left.

6.
Aligning
your golf sights

TO COMPLETE THE FULL AND ACCURATE body alignment, it is necessary to jump ahead in our instruction and
act as if we already know the proper grip.

We know how the body must be placed for the perfect
address position, but what happens in actual play? How
can you be sure that, although you have the perfect
address position, you are lined up properly?

There is a way that is almost foolproof. First, give your
eyes an alignment check. You can give yourself this
alignment check while out on the golf course. Use the
flag on the green as your target. If indoors, select any
small object in your room, something about the size of a
golf ball. A door knob will do. After having picked your
target turn your back to it. While your back is turned,
hold a golf club at arm's length and shoulder height
directly in front of you, with both hands apart, width of
shoulders, on the clubshaft—the right hand near the clubhead and the left hand near the clubhandle.

Now make believe that you are holding a rifle in your
hands instead of a golf club. Then turn and, without disturbing the extension of your arms, adjust your imaginary

rifle so that it is lined up to send an imaginary bullet to your target. When you feel that you have your club (imaginary rifle) lined up exactly on the target, let go of the shaft with your left hand. Without moving the position of the shaft or the position of the right hand, hold the shaft extended in the air with the right hand until you are able to check the alignment of the shaft on the target by stepping in back of the shaft and looking down it as you would a rifle. You will be very much surprised to see at how far off you are in your alignment.

Do not be alarmed, for most people are off in this right angle alignment one way or another. If you were holding the shaft as though it were a rifle, in the conventional way, it would be a very simple matter to line up your target accurately. But holding it out at arm's length presents another problem and this is exactly what takes place when you try to line up a ball to your target while you are standing in a side position in relation to your target, as in the address position.

It is even more difficult than shooting at arm's length for the ball will be farther away than the distance of your extended arms. But do not fret as there is a way that this problem can be overcome once and for all. First, however, you must find out which is your master eye.

For the benefit of those who do not know which is the master eye, or those who have not read my book, *Secrets of Accurate Putting and Chipping,* in which I explain the master eye, I shall very quickly explain what it is. If you already know which is your master eye, it would not hurt you to quickly re-check it to make sure you are correct.

With both eyes open point your right forefinger at any small object approximately twenty feet away. With your finger pointing to the object close one eye, and then the other, and you will notice your finger move. The eye that lines up the finger closest to your target is the master eye.

In most cases a right-handed person's master eye is his right eye and a left-handed person's master eye is his left. The eye that keeps your finger on the target is the master eye. It is the master eye that gives the correct alignment for all acts in which proper direction is needed.

While your master eye determines direction, your other eye determines depth or distance. This eye is called the "depth eye." The point where they meet is called the point of *central fixation.* When you look at a photograph or a store window your brain sees only one image, and that image is clearest only at the point of central fixation.

In order to see the picture or object (that is, the green, the flag, or cup) more clearly, you should blink your eyes a few times. Then focus them on various sections of the

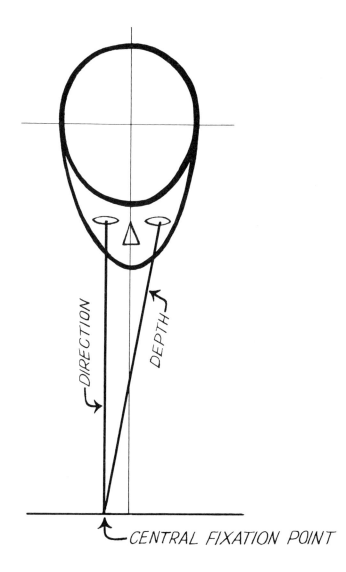

DIRECTION

DEPTH

CENTRAL FIXATION POINT

71

object you are looking at. In this way your brain receives more mental pictures and your vision becomes clearer. As a result, you will be able to see clearly details that you could not see before. On the green you will be able to see even the slightest slopes and undulations.

When striving for direction, favor your master eye; when distance is paramount, favor your depth eye. In favoring an eye, merely think that this particular eye is dominant or doing the most work.

I suggest you do the exercise to strengthen your eyes. A very good eye exercise is found in the last chapter of this book.

In lining yourself up for a full shot, stand in back of the ball so that your master eye directly in a line to the ball and from the ball to the intended target. In lining up use both eyes—for not only do you need direction but a gauge of distance is also necessary.

Now while standing in back of the ball glance down at your hands and get your grip on your clubhandle. Remember we are jumping ahead in our instruction since I have not yet shown you the proper hold. Make sure that you do this while the clubhead is resting on the ground, for you would not get an accurate hold if you took your grip while the clubhead is in the air. There would be a faulty alignment of clubface in relation to your hands.

After you get the proper hold on the club, raise the clubhead off the ground and then, while holding the clubhead in the air with the proper grip, again check the line in which you want your ball to travel.

While still looking at and facing your target, walk over to the approximate area of where you would stand to address the ball.

If, in walking to the approximate area of where you are going to stand, you take your eyes off the target, you will lose your accurate alignment. You must walk with your eyes focused on your target and then, while still facing the target, trace a visual line from the target to the ball. When you focus your eyes on the ball, mentally let the depth eye take over, for this is the one you will use during your swing. Look at the ball casually with both eyes open, with just the thought that the depth eye is in control. Then, without concentrating on the position of your body, place the clubface carefully in back of the ball, in its natural lie, at a perfect right angle to the intended line of flight.

Without moving the angle of the clubface, place your left foot carefully in the proper relation to the position of the clubface and ball. Place your right foot in the proper relation to your left foot, making sure as you do that the line of your heels is parallel with the intended line of flight. Adjust your legs, trunk, shoulders, arms and hands properly, in this order, in relation to the correct angle of the clubface.

You are now in perfect alignment with your target. I must warn you that it may look off line to you but trust this first alignment even though it may look wrong. If you readjust yourself, you will get yourself all out of line. Trust

Aligning your golf sights

your first alignment and you will seldom go wrong.

However, if you feel absolutely sure that it is not quite correct, you must start all over from the beginning and go through the proper order of movements. Keep this order of movements in aligning your body for all shots and you will begin to develop greater consistency.

Order of Movements

(1) Get your correct line.

(2) Get the correct hold on the club.

(3) Place clubface at perfect right angle to the intended line of flight.

(4) Favor the depth eye.

(5) Carefully adjust left foot in the proper relation to clubface and ball.

(6) Adjust right foot in proper relation to left foot.

(7) Adjust legs, trunk, shoulders, arms, and hands to fit the position of the clubhead.

While you go through this order of movements, you must not move or change the position of the clubface. Otherwise, the result will be a faulty alignment.

Sequence for acquiring the proper alignment of shot. A. Stand
with master eye directly in back of ball. Get grip while clubhead is resting naturally on ground, never while club is in air.

B. While still looking at line of target, lift clubhead in cocking manner.

C. While holding wrists cocked and still looking at target and without taking eyes off target, walk over to the approximate area of ball.

D. While still facing the target, follow the imaginary line from the target back to the ball, and then place the face of clubhead at perfect right angles to the intended line of flight.

E. Then carefully place the left foot in its proper relation to the clubface and ball, being careful not to move the position of the clubface. You have now established a physical contact with the ball, eliminating the guess work as to the distance you should stand from the ball.

F. Then carefully place the right foot in its proper relation to the left foot, then adjust the alignment of your shoulders and arms to make sure that they are on a line to the right of your target. You are now in perfect alignment and ready to fire (swing). At times after you are lined up, it may feel to you as though you are a bit off line, do not let this trick of right angle vision throw you off, trust this alignment as it will usually be correct. If you still feel that it is incorrect, then start all over and make sure that it is correct. Do not worry about the length of time it takes you to align yourself, as this is the most important phase of your swing.

G. Heels will be lined up to the left of the target. The clubface will be at a perfect right angle to the intended line of flight. The line of the shoulders and arms will be pointing to the right of the target along the same path that you expect your club-head to travel through as it meets the ball.

7.
The four swings of golf

WHAT ARE YOU SCORING? ARE YOU IN THE 70's, 80's, 90's, or can't you break 100?

Why is it that after a considerable amount of time and effort, you have not improved as much as you should?

Here is one of the main reasons. Let us assume you are having trouble breaking 100. You seek the help of a professional. The professional is an excellent golfer. He shoots in the low 70's and, at times, in the 60's. The professional's golf swing, after many years of practice and hard work, has evolved and developed to its present high degree of skill. What does a person who is extremely skillful think of in the performing of a skilled physical act? In terms of muscular execution, practically nothing.

The skilled golfer is not thinking of what muscle to use or what position his body must be in at such and such a section of his swing. Most of his attention is concentrated on where he wants the ball to end up. However, he may have one or two key points that he checks in regard to his alignment, but seldom more. The less attention the skilled golfer gives to himself while swinging, the greater is his degree of skill.

The golfer who is struggling to break 100 is thinking and swinging in terms of someone who is trying to break 100. The professional is thinking and swinging in terms of someone who is shooting in the low 70's and at times in the 60's.

If the professional were to teach the advanced swing and techniques that he is using to the fellow who is struggling to break 100 the result would be confusion and little or no progress. These two people, the professional and the high-scoring player, are in two different worlds of skill. The high-scoring individual is not mentally nor physically prepared to accept and transpose into a physical act any of the advanced instructions that he would receive.

The instructor may be very honest and sincere in explaining the techniques that he is using in swinging a golf club. Unfortunately, this would be of little help to the struggling golfer. In order to reach the understanding of the pupil so that he can eventually show some real improvement, the instructor must exert enough imagination to step back in his golfing skill so as to put himself at the student's level of understanding and skill.

The four swings of golf

At times this simple fact is overlooked. It is a pity, for it is the only way in which the pupil can truly be helped.

There are actually four swings in golf and each swing has its own mental interpretation of execution.

(1) The mental interpretation and swinging of a person trying to break 100.

(2) The mental interpretation and swinging of someone trying to break 90.

(3) The mental interpretation and swinging of someone trying to break 80.

(4) The mental attitude and swinging of the golfer shooting in the low 70's and, occasionally, in the 60's.

What we have gone through to this point are the basic essentials all golfers must have in every bracket of skill. The basic understanding and the correctness of alignment in the proper address, plus the proper finish position, are the necessary preparatory foundations upon which can be built the highest brackets of skill in golf.

If you did nothing more than what we have gone through in this book up to this point, your golf swing and understanding of basic principles should be at a pitch of skill high enough to eventually break 90. But let us not be satisfied just yet; with a little more effort and understanding, your pitch of skill can rise immeasurably.

The next magical bracket of skill we shall call The Key to the Master Golf Swing.

8.
The key to
the master
golf swing

WHAT IS TRUE CENTRIFUGAL FORCE? IT IS ENERGY starting out in one direction and then curving off at a tangent. It is energy going away from the center of rotation. You may remember, when you were a child, how you marveled at what kept the water from spilling out when you swung a pail of water over your head.

The energy that keeps the water in the pail is called centrifugal force. It is energy going away from the center of rotation. In swinging the pail of water with your arm your shoulder resists the centrifugal force. If you did not have a center that resists or an energy that pulls towards its center, or any fixed point that holds its center, you could not have centrifugal force. This energy, or center, that holds or resists the centrifugal force, is called the "centripetal point." You cannot have centrifugal force unless you have a centripetal point.

The power that can be developed by the centripetal and centrifugal forces are tremendous, enough to even hold the earth in its orbit, enough to increase the pull of gravity many times, as is proven by an airplane pilot coming out of a dive. This energy has been at our disposal since the beginning of time. This is the tremendous force that will be transposed into your golf swing. Fortunately, it is a simple matter to perform, for the key to the development of this energy is understanding.

As I stated before, you never have centrifugal force without a centripetal point. The centripetal point of your golf swing is *the base of your spine*. The position of your right leg, in the course of your backswing, determines whether the centripetal point remains at the base of your spine, where it should be, or is dissipated and wasted in the course of your swing.

The right leg, which we shall call "the key to the master golf swing," is the most important single item in building a swing that can generate tremendous force with the maximum of consistency. If, on the way back, your right leg is not at the correct angle, the rest of the body can never be quite right.

Here is how you can find the correct position for yourself. Stand in the address position so that your right side is facing a wall or a stick stuck straight up on your right. Stand so that your right foot is up against and touching the wall or stick. Note how many inches your right thigh, in the area of your right pocket, is from the wall or stick on your right. On the way back in your backswing this distance must remain the same, neither getting closer nor farther away.

As you turn back in your backswing, your right leg must remain at the same angle that it was in during the address position.

You will find that the greatest golfers in the world have this one point in common. There may be a slight variation in the rest of their swings but in this one point, the angle of the right leg at the top of the backswing, it is the same. *It is a must for great golf.*

Many descriptions have been given of this point. Some would say "swing as though you are standing in a barrel." That is close but not quite correct, for in a barrel your right thigh can still shift to the right those few, vital inches. I believe that standing against the stick or wall with your right foot touching the wall or stick will give you a most accurate measurement.

Practice the feel of this position without a golf club starting from the address. Make sure that, on the way back, your right leg remains at the exact same angle at which you started. It may feel as though you are shifting your weight toward your right in your endeavor to attain the correct position with your right thigh. If it feels this way, accept it—for there is no set rule as to the feeling you should have. As all individuals are built differently, the trick is to find your own feeling for getting into this correct leg position.

Position A. First step in exercise for preparation for acquiring the heart or centripetal point in the golf swing. Weight is equally divided on both feet. Center of heels apart the width of the hips.

Position B. Turn shoulders and upper body toward right. Right leg must remain at the same angle as in the start.

(Exercise 2.)

Bow toward right from waist. Do not disturb angle of right leg. Familiarize yourself with this position as it is the correct body position at the point of return (or as it is called, the top of the backswing, Position #2). By bowing to the right you will be preparing for what is to follow.

The key to the master golf swing

With the correct right leg position your swing will also begin to tighten up and become more compact. Try a few swings in your own way from the address position to the finish, keeping the correct right leg position in mind. The right leg remains at this position from the address to the top of the backswing only. From then on forget about the right leg. Keeping the right leg at the correct angle on the way back is the only way to acquire a true centripetal pont. When you have mastered the correct leg position to the point where you can repeat it at will, you can then continue building the swing with the assurance that your foundation is absolutely correct.

9.
Reaching for power

THE NEXT MOST VITAL POSITION IN THE MASTER golf swing is the position of your body from the waist up at the completion of the backswing. Let's delve into this.

Many years ago two scales were placed under the feet of a top golfer in order to find out where the majority of his weight rested during the top of the backswing. They found that the greater part of the weight was registered under the right foot.

There is more weight on the right foot at the top of the backswing—*but* a very significant point was overlooked.

During the course of learning a pupil is often asked to shift his weight to the right on the way back and then to the left on the way through. In doing this the body sometimes sways. To correct the sway, the pupil is asked to keep his head still while swinging. Now, how in the world can you keep your head still while you are shifting your body weight to the right on the way back, and then to the left in the follow-through? If, on the backswing, you kept your head still and shifted your weight to the right, the result at the top of the backswing would be a position of very little power and very little consistency.

The poor, struggling golfer, in an effort to keep his head still, finds that he can do so without too much shifting of the weight and, eventually, he eliminates most of the weight shifting. Finally, after many years of playing, the body starts to pivot properly of its own accord. The golfer, after struggling for so long a time and although getting better results by not shifting his weight, feels that he is not swinging quite right and that there is a terrible fault in his swing. So, regardless of his success, there will always be some doubt and therefore he can never be as good as he should be.

How often have you heard someone say to a duffer who has just missed a shot that he moved or lifted his head? We now know how ridiculous that is. It is impossible to take a natural full swing without moving your head.

Let us clear the confusion once and for all as to what is the correct position of the body from the waist up at the top of the backswing. The scales proved that the weight should go to the right. Yes, but what caused the majority of the weight to register on the right scale?

We know the correct position of the right leg at the

Reaching for power

top of the backswing. This position will give you the
centripetal point in your golf swing. But what about
the body from the waist up? The proper handling of
the body from the waist up is one of the major factors responsible for giving modern golfers such tremendous
length off the tee. Immediately following the proper
placing of the right leg, the correct placement of the
body from the waist up is the next most important position
in golf anatomy. The better it is understood, the easier it
will be learned and performed.

On the following pages notice the negatives of the three
golfers at the top of their backswings. When a golfer is
told to shift his weight to the right on the backswing, he
looks something like Golfer A. On page 96 notice that
although he will be able to create a very large circle, as
on page 97, there is no center or centripetal point in his
swing. His right leg has lost its perfect position and has
swayed way over to the right. He can hit a few good shots
once in a while with the body in this position, but a great
many bad shots will also be hit. You can learn to play this
way but you can never develop the great degree of skill
and consistency that you are truly capable of.

Notice Golfers B and C on pages 98 and 99. In both
cases the right leg is in the correct position. Both golfers
have a center or centripetal point. Now check the position,
from the waist up, of Golfer B. This position was typical
of the golfers of many years ago. They had great accuracy
but with the upper body in this position, the greatest
length could not be obtained. Why is this so? Notice that

Golfer B, from the waist up, is leaning back—thereby making the circle that he is creating with his clubhead not quite as large as it could be, resulting in loss of power; for the greater the circle, the greater the clubhead speed.

Look at Golfer C on p. 100. Here is your modern golfer. Whether he realizes it or not, he is bowing forward and reaching out at the waist, enabling himself to create as large an arc as possible. The correct position of his right leg maintains the centripetal point. Notice that, with the body leaning over to the right from the waist up, the weight at the top of the backswing is now more on the right foot.

In the perfect swing it is actually the leaning over to the right of the body from the waist up that gives you the weight on your right, and not the shifting to the right of the entire body. Now you may say that this will cause you to sway. This is not so, for swaying is moving away from the center. As long as you keep your right leg in its centripetal point position, it is impossible to sway.

Upon getting into the proper trunk position it will seem as though you are moving your head excessively toward the right. Yes, your head will move toward the right. This is correct but actually you will not be moving as much as you think. The movement of the head toward the right in the backswing will seem great because your eyes are focused on the ball. When your eyes are focused on a fixed point, any movement of the head can be very easily felt. A fellow shooting a rifle, who has his eyes fixed on his gunsight and aligned with his target, will notice a great deal of movement in his rifle; the onlooker will seem to feel that the rifleman's head and rifle are stationary.

Golfer A. Incorrect. Body out of line, therefore centripetal
point is lost. Very little accuracy.

Golfer A. Showing fairly large circle. Very little accuracy, as
centripetal point is lost.

Golfer B. Golfer leaning back thereby shortening radius. Accuracy with little power.

Golfer B. Showing small radius—good center, accuracy, little power.

Golfer C. Showing great extension of arc creating more power
right leg maintains centripetal point giving accuracy. Body
leans over giving greater width which adds to greater power.

notice a great deal of movement in his rifle; the onlooker will seem to feel that the rifleman's head and rifle are stationary.

Do not worry about the amount of head movement you seem to be getting, for after practicing this position a few times, you will soon become accustomed to this movement and it will feel very natural.

Another good way of getting into this proper body position at the top of the backswing, is to get the impression that you are going to throw a baseball overhand, starting from the address position to a full windup on the way back. With this in mind you will notice that your body will instinctively fall into the correct position.

I must warn you of two pitfalls that you can get into on the way back in your backswing. One of these concerns your left hip. On the way back the hip must not be lowered. If the left hip dips lower than the position it was in during the address, then a great deal of power will be lost. The lowering of the hip will influence the centripetal point in your swing and will also affect the position of the body from the waist up. On the way back, keep your left hip high and another degree of power and accuracy will be added to your swing.

What causes the left hip to drop in the course of your backswing? Notice, as you take your backswing, that your left knee will bend in toward the ball so as to allow the body to pivot more freely. If the heel of the left foot remains down, your backswing will be restricted. Also, keeping the heel down will cause you to collapse in the area of the left hip and put your body in a very weak position through the loss of the centripetal point. As you take your backswing, the left heel, without changing the angle of the left foot, must come up high enough to keep the left hip at the same height it was in during the address position.

Actually, both hips should remain high and on a level plane, with neither the left nor the right hip slipping in the process of the backswing.

The other pitfall, the one causing a great deal of trouble, is the path your left shoulder takes as you go into your backswing.

Although you may have been made to believe that it is correct for the left shoulder to drop or dip in the course of the backswing, unfortunately it is *another* mistaken interpretation of what the correct anatomical position should be at the top of the backswing.

Unlike the position of the right leg (as it creates the centripetal point) good golf can be played with the left shoulder in the dipped or down position and many good golfers are in this position at the top of their backswings. But with their left shoulders in this down position, their greatest power and highest degree of skill could not be developed. The best golf is played by golfers who keep their left shoulders up at the top of their backswings.

This position will give the body a tremendous power release and a consistency that is almost uncanny. The lack of this one point, the up-ness of the left shoulder at the top of the backswing, prevents many of our fine players from becoming truly great.

The left shoulder does not drop or rise, but goes back level in the course of the backswing.

To test the correctness of this shoulder position, try this experiment. Take a backswing with your left shoulder dropping. Then stop at the top of this backswing. While in this position let go of your golf club and let it fall to the ground. Imagine yourself throwing a baseball, with your right hand, overhand toward the target, or green, from this position. You will find that it would be almost impossible to throw a baseball overhand with any great force. Then raise your left shoulder and you will immediately feel a sense of greater power. Notice that with your left shoulder down in your backswing you lose the extension and greatness of the arc.

In delivering great force, the expert baseball pitcher, hammer thrower, discus thrower, baseball batter, javelin thrower, tennis player, skilled boxer, the expert shot-putter, and many other athletes at the completion of the windup or backswing, will have their left shoulder higher than their right.

For a position of maximum power and consistency on the way back, both the left hip and the left shoulder must travel back along the same level and height they were in during the address position. This is an absolute rule.

Reaching for power

Do not go to the other extreme and lift your left shoulder too high. If you did you would lose sight of the ball and it would cause your body to straighten up too much, destroying the depth distance from the Adam's apple to the ball.

How much should the shoulder be allowed to turn on the way back? Each person has a limitation of flexibility.

Let the left shoulder turn back as far as it will go with comfort and not destroy the position of the right leg. You can give yourself a good gauge as to how far back your shoulder should turn by keeping your left eye focused on the ball on the way back and letting your left shoulder continue turning until you can see the left shoulder go past the ball. Then you will know that you have enough turn. A full turn of the shoulder on the way back will also put you in a position making it easier for the clubhead to come through on the correct in-to-out path. With an insufficient amount of shoulder turn on the way back the shoulders would be in a position to help induce an incorrect out-to-in path.

Here is a little exercise (shown on page 106) that will help you learn the proper leg and trunk position at the top of the backswing.

Stand up straight with your right side to a wall far enough away so that you can stretch your right arm until the fingers of your right hand touch the wall on your right. Now step still farther away from the wall until your outstretched fingers are at least 10 inches from the wall

Reaching for power

Turn as in the backswing and, without destroying the position of the right leg (the centripetal point), reach over and touch the wall with the fingers of your left hand. Repeat this exercise 10 times each morning and in a little while you will be amazed at the power you will be getting in your golf swing.

It is not a bad idea to do some of these exercises each morning as setting-up exercises. They will not only help you keep fit but will also help your golf swing. Later on I shall give you a complete set of golf exercises that can be done in a few minutes and will be beneficial both to your golf swing and to your well-being.

Exercise showing touching wall will help get you into the
perfect position at point of return.

Point of return Position #2. Right leg maintains the centripetal point. Upper body is bowing over thereby increasing the radius of your swing. Left shoulder has not dipped. Left pelvis (or hip) is high. Left arm is extended. Wrists are fully cocked. Depth eye is looking at ball. All forces are ready to be unleashed at ball.

10.
How to hold
a golf club

NOW THAT YOU HAVE A CLEARER UNDERSTANDING of what the correct body position should be at the top of the backswing, let us continue developing the swing by working on the arms and hands.

In order to get the proper understanding of how the hands should be placed on the club, we must first be sure that the arms are in the correct position. In order to do that, we must step back in our learning to the ape position.

Assume the ape position (slightly bowed over at the waist, with your arms hanging down relaxed). Note the angle of your left hand as it hangs down limply. Each person's left hand will rest at an angle to fit his or her particular type of build.

When the hand is allowed to hang down completely relaxed in a limp state at your side there is no pronation of that hand. What is hand pronation? Let us find out.

Place your left hand and arm, up to the elbow, palm down with the fingers outstretched on any table or flat surface. If the palm and fingers of your hand are lying flat against the surface, then there is no hand pronation. Now lift your hand 4 inches above the flat surface leaving the elbow still touching the surface. If the palm of your hand is still facing the flat surface as it was when it was

RADIUS

ULNA

NO-PRONATION

PRONATION
(RADIUS CROSSES ULNA)

PALM
DOWN

resting against the surface, you still have no pronation. But if you turn the hand to the left or to the right so that the palm is no longer facing the flat surface, your hand is now in a position of pronation. If you make a complete turn until the palm is facing upward you have full pronation. The degree of turn determines the amount of pronation.

In our forearm we have two bones called the ulna and the radius. In the act of pronation these two bones cross over one another, robbing us of maximum sensitivity. Pronation is usually a movement that you, yourself, consciously perform. The trick is to find out at what angle your left hand is in while it is hanging relaxed, for this is the angle your hand should be in as it holds the club.

Leaving the left hand where it is, as it hangs down in the ape position as on pages 113 and 114, place a golf club in your left hand but as you place the club imagine that the handle of the club is not round, but square. As you place it in your left hand, you will find that your left thumb will be resting lightly on the top right corner of this (square) handle. This position will be correct for you.

Should the handle be held by the fingers or in the palm of your left hand? There is no set rule as to where the handle should be held, for no two people have hands that are alike. If you have long fingers, then the handle will instinctively be held mainly by the fingers. If you have short fingers, the handle will be held in the palm of the hand.

Just grasp the clubhandle with your left hand naturally, paying no attention to whether your clubhandle is in the fingers or in the palm of the left hand. Make sure, though, that you do not change the angle of the left hand for this is the most important part of the grip. As long as you do no conscious turning of the left hand as you hold the club-handle, you have the correct hold with your left hand.

The same applies to the right hand—there should not be any pronation or turning.

Let us continue the development of the grip by placing the right hand on the handle properly.

Leaving your left hand holding the club, without pronating or turning the angle of your right hand, bring the right hand down and over toward the left hand. Place the right hand on the shaft handle underneath the left hand, so that the right hand is not touching the left. While doing this make sure that your right elbow is bent and hugging close to the right side of your body. If you place the right hand on the imaginary square handle without turning the angle of your right hand, you will find that the right thumb will be resting on the top left hand corner of the imaginary square handle.

You will notice that the right hand, in reaching over to the left to hold the handle, will instinctively hold the club with a tendency toward the fingers. Both hands are apart and if, in swinging, you leave them apart there would be a battle for supremacy; the stronger hand, usually the right (in the case of a right-handed golfer) would overpower the left hand. This is not good, for both hands should work together as a single unit.

In order to equalize the strength of both hands, lift the little finger of the right hand off the clubhandle and keep it off. This weakens the right hand somewhat, and equalizes the amount of pressure from both hands. While the little finger of the right hand is still off the clubhandle, without letting go of the handle, slide your right hand toward your left until the heel and the fingers of the right hand are pressing firmly against the left.

The right little finger is still standing out. In order to make one complete unit of both hands bring this finger down, and rest it on the fingers of the left hand. There is no set rule as to where this little finger should be. It depends on the size and shape of the individual's hands. Let it naturally close, as in making a fist, and the little finger will find its own resting place as on page 117.

There should be no space between the fingers of either hand and the right palm should be resting firmly against the left thumb. The closer together the hands are the better.

You have often heard it said that you must point both V's of your hand to your right shoulder. Well, let's find out.

If the hands, when placed on the clubhandle in their

natural position with no pronation or turning, end up with the so-called V's pointing to the right shoulder, then it is correct. But if you must consciously turn either or both hands over one way or the other to get this effect, *then it is absolutely wrong.* For there is no rule that says that these two V's must point to the right shoulder. Wherever the hands end up naturally, when they are placed on the club without pronation, is the correct placement for you.

If you force your hands to get the V's to point towards the right shoulder the brain must send down a conscious line of thought to the base of the spine, back to the brain, and then to the muscle used.

This conscious line of thought must be retained throughout your entire swing. If you break it your hands will leave their original position, causing the clubface to turn thereby giving you a poor hit.

Because of this conscious awareness of the degree of pronation, your wrists will not have the freedom or flexibility they should. You could never have your arms and hands relaxed. The less attention given, the higher the degree of skill will be.

In getting the proper hold on the golf club, both hands must be free of turning or pronation.

Practice this placement of your hands on the club until you can do it almost instinctively, then we shall be prepared to go on to another step on the ladder of skill.

In acquiring the proper grip make sure the left arm and left hand do not turn (pronate) either way. Then, leaving the left hand where it is, place the clubhandle in the left hand.

Angle of left arm and left hand remains as it was during the Ape Position while the arm was hanging down limply. As to whether the club should be held in the fingers or palm, there is no set rule for this. If you have long fingers the club will naturally be in the fingers. If you have short fingers, the club will naturally be held in the palm. The important part is to be sure the left arm and left hand remain at the same angle they were in during the relaxed state.

Right hand goes over to meet the left hand. Club is held in
fingers of right hand.

The completed grip. Both hands are fused together into a single unit. There is no set rule as to where the V's of both hands should point. Wherever they end up naturally is the correct spot for you. Hold with hands should be light as though you were holding a bird in your hands. You would not crush it, and yet you would not let if fly away. Wrists must be loose and relaxed.

Little finger of right hand overlaps forefinger of left hand so that both hands become fused into one unit and not into separate forces.

11.
Starting
your swing

WE WILL NOW LEARN THE CORRECT WAY OF starting the anatomical engine of your golf swing so that you can be sure you are in the correct position at the top of your backswing. There is a manner of starting back which puts you in the perfect position of maximum power and accuracy at the top and it requires only the minimum of attention in the early stages of your learning. Once learned, it will repeat itself instinctively.

Get yourself in the correct address position. When everything is aligned properly and you are looking at the ball with your depth eye while holding the golf club in your hands, squeeze both hands together as though you were wringing a towel. You do this by turning the right hand toward the left, and the left hand toward the right, without letting the hands slip on the club. At this point the hands should be tight and firm.

Now relax both hands and let them return to the original position on the club. This tightening and the relaxation will show you the difference between a firm hold and a light hold. In holding the handle properly throughout the entire swing, the light hold should be used. You should hold the club as lightly as though you were holding a little bird in your hands. You would not crush it and yet you would not want to let it fly away. It should feel as if you were holding the club only with the skin of your hands.

Add a little more pressure with your left hand—enough to enable you to lift the weight of the golf club off the ground. This is the ultimate amount of pressure and strength that should be exerted with your left hand in your golf swing. As for your right hand, it should remain relaxed on the handle.

A good way of knowing what the feeling of your right hand should be like, is to imagine you are holding a pistol and that you are aiming this gun at the ball. Your right forefinger is on the trigger of the pistol. Let us assume that this pistol has an extremely light and sensitive trigger pull. Very little pressure should be exerted with your right index finger or the gun will go off.

The right hand should hold the handle mainly with the thumb and forefinger with enough pressure to make you aware of their position. Once aware, take your attention away from your right hand and you will have the correct hold with this hand.

Starting your swing

As I said before the left hand should exert just a little more pressure on the handle than your right—enough to be able to lift the weight of the golf club as you take your backswing.

If you straighten up by raising your back, the left hand which will be holding the club with enough strength will allow the club to rise off the ground. Raise and lower the club head a few inches off the ground (using your back, *not* your arms). Lower the clubhead back to its original position. This raising and lowering of your back will enable you to measure your depth more accurately.

Actually this raising and lowering has many advantages. It is used as an accurate depth gauge, as an aid to proper alignment and relaxation, and also as the key to the starting of your golf (engine) swing.

This shall be our method of waggle—the club going up and down with your back rather than, as is customary, to waggle from side to side by using your hands and wrists. Do this up and down waggle only a few times, rarely more than three times before each swing. On the last waggle, when the clubhead is on its last journey on the way down back to its original position in back of the ball, the instant after the clubhead touches the ground in its proper alignment is the time to start your backswing.

The backswing starts with a movement that is known as the forward press. A forward press is a very slight movement of a part of the body in one direction, in preparation for a major movement of the body in the opposite direction. The forward press is a very important and necessary part of the golf swing and when you become more skillful, it will automatically get your swing started properly, eliminating a great deal of tension. Freezing up at the start of the golf swing is extremely detrimental, for this is when you must have the greatest trust in your golf swing.

You need something to help you get started properly and the forward press comes in very handy. It can be done with almost any part of the body—the hands, arms, shoulders, hips, feet. It can be a slight pause or it can even be just a mental movement.

The forward press that we shall use will be the forward press of the feet. This press starts the instant after the clubhead is set in its proper place in back of the ball at the end of the last waggle.

At this moment both your feet should become alert. Then your right foot should take over and gently turn your relaxed hips very slightly toward the left. This movement should be so slight as to be almost inperceptible.

It should feel as though it were done to alert your feet to the fact that they are going to play a very important part in the golf swing. It should feel as if a mental transference of body weight from the right foot to the left foot were taking place; as though a message were being sent from your right foot to the left foot in order to awaken the left foot so that it can begin its job.

Then, without pausing, let your left foot take over and

push the relaxed left hip. This moves the right hip smartly and sharply back to the right, in the opposite direction of the forward press. It should feel as if the forward press and the start back are one and the same movement.

As your left foot pushes your left hip around toward the right, the left hip, the left shoulder, the left arm, the left hand, and the clubhead should go back together at the same time and at the same rate of speed. This whole turn originates in the feet. The feet cause the hips to turn. The hips cause the shoulders to turn. The shoulders cause the extended left arm, the left hand, the clubshaft, and the clubhead to go back together and in the proper path of the backswing. The path that the clubhead goes into naturally is the correct path the clubhead should take.

Make sure that the hips and shoulders, in the process of the backswing, go back on the level plane that we discussed earlier so that you do not dip the hips. Otherwise, you cannot get into the proper position at the top of the backswing.

On the way back, the feet and the hips will be the first to complete their turn before any other part of the body since the feet cause the hips to wind up. The hips, on the way back, carry the shoulders which, in turn, carry the arms, hands, and the clubhead. When the hips have reached the limit of their full turn and have carried the shoulders, arms, hands, and the clubhead part of the way back, the hips stop turning. The shoulders then take over, continuing the turn back carrying the arms, hands, and the clubhead. When the shoulders have reached their full wind-up, the shoulders stop and the arms take over.

Before we continue it is imperative to explain the proper function of the left arm.

Resume the address position. Note that in the correct address position, the left arm is hanging extended and the right arm is bent in at the elbow. Both hands are in the proper hold position on the golf handle.

There is a protrusion on the top of the left side of the left wrist just at the point where the arm ends and the wrist begins. It is called the styloid process. It is on the end of the ulna in the left arm. If you cannot seem to find this point in the left wrist area, choose the spot in the left wrist where you would ordinarily wear a wrist watch. Use the strap of the wrist watch as your point of measure.

If you were to point with an extended left arm, the distance from the wrist bone to the top of the shoulder bone would be at its greatest. The arm is fully extended and yet relaxed. In holding the golf club in the proper address position, the distance from the left knob of the ulna to the top of the left shoulder bone should also be at its greatest. In order to attain the highest degree of clubhead speed and consistency, you must maintain the distance from the left wrist bone to the top of the left shoulder bone throughout the backswing, downswing, and as far past the actual hitting of the ball as is physically possible for you.

The maintenance of the maximum distance should be

accomplished with as little effort and with as much relaxation as possible. Otherwise, the shoulder and the left arm muscles will tighten up and there will be a great loss of clubhead speed and accuracy.

If, on the way back, you shorten the distance from the left wrist to the top of the left shoulder bone, you not only reduce the radius of your arc, losing clubhead speed and accuracy, but also most of the force generated from the feet and up through the body will seep out at the left elbow. And most of the power of the perfect windup will be wasted.

You may say that because of your type build you cannot keep your left arm straight at the top of the backswing. I did not say that the left arm should be straight. I said it should maintain a relaxed extension, an extension so delicate that the extension is the result of the weight of the left hand itself pulling the relaxed arm, as when you take up the slack in a fishing line and allow the weight at the end of the line to keep the line taut.

A more forceful example of weight pulling the arm would be if you were to imagine yourself carrying a heavy suitcase in your left hand for any great length of time. Your left arm would be extended, but relaxed, for it would be the weight of the suitcase that would keep the arm extended. There would be no necessity for the major muscle of the left arm (the biceps) to be used. Strength would only be exerted in the left hand and just enough strength to hold the suitcase. The shoulder bone would be supporting most of the weight of the suitcase, and the rest of the body would be supporting the shoulder bone.

If the left arm is held extended in this relaxed manner, you will find that the left arm and the area of the left shoulder has a freedom and vitality that is almost unbelievable. When you move the left arm let the mental focal point of movement originate in the area of the left wrist bone. This is the type of freedom that we need in the golf swing. Each person has his or her limitation of left arm extension. The trick is to keep the arm extended as much as is physically possible for you.

You may say, "Yes, I can keep the left arm fairly extended in the address position, but what about at the top of the backswing?"

Actually, you should be able to keep the left arm extended at the top of the backswing to the same degree it is at the address position. The reason most people have trouble with this part of the golf swing is because of a lack of true understanding of body mechanics. Give yourself this little test.

Assume the address position with the club, ball and all. Without using your hips, turn the shoulders around as in the backswing—just the shoulders, not the hips. Let the shoulders carry the arms, hands and clubhead just as far as the shoulders can go. Do this a few times and notice the path the clubhead takes on the way back as it leaves the position of rest in back of the ball. As you already know, this is the proper path that the clubhead should take, not only for this experiment, but for the regular golf swing.

This time, while keeping the left arm extended as it was in the address position, without moving the shoulders, let the extended left arm go back as far as it can, carrying the clubhead along the proper path—without moving the shoulders, bending or destroying the extension of the left arm, and without any cocking of the wrists.

Keep going back until you can go no further. You will notice that the movement of the left arm has not been as much as you thought. This is the limit of your arm backswing for your particular type of build.

It is the turning of the shoulders that acts as the barometer of the length of the backswing. Some golfers try to take a full backswing with very little or no shoulder turn. This is not correct as the radius of the swing must be destroyed in order to allow the left arm to go farther *back* than the turn of the shoulders will allow. The left arm must collapse at the elbow. This is not desirable for it destroys the width of the arc.

If you feel that you cannot keep the left arm extended at the top of the backswing, check your shoulder turn, as this is usually the cause of the restriction.

After the end of the shoulder turn is completed and the left arm has completed its backward and upward journey in the backswing, you should find your left arm in the area above the right shoulder and below the right ear. It does not have to be exactly between these two points. Anywhere between the right shoulder and the right ear is correct. Some of the top golfers are closer to the right shoulder. Others are closer to the right ear. Your body will find its own particular position.

What about the right arm?

If you do nothing with the right arm but keep it completely relaxed on the way back, and let the left arm influence the position of the right arm, it will end up in the right place.

Complete relaxation also means no concentration on the particular part of the body involved. After you set your right arm in the correct address position at the start, do not pay any attention to it. It will behave properly. (Herein I have just given you a clue to one of the secrets of physical skill.)

Briefly, what we have accomplished so far in the backswing is this:

From the address position the feet turn the hips. The hips turn the shoulders. The shoulders direct and move the arms back. The left wrist bone continues the arm back to its proper place. What about the hands and wrists?

Well, we can now go on to a discussion of the part the hands and the wrists play in the golf swing.

12.
Proper use of wrist and hands

ACTUALLY I COULD NOT FIX YOUR HANDS UNTIL I first adjusted your arms. Proper arm adjustment depends *on* the correct placement of your shoulders, just as the position of the shoulders depends on the working position of your hips, knees and feet.

Suppose the large part of the body was like the motor of an automobile. The arms are the carburetor. The wrist and hands are the adjustment screws on the carburetor. I would not be able to make a correct carburetor (wrist and hand) adjustment until the rest of the motor was in fine working order.

Before we are ready for the key to the ultimate degree of skill (supplying brain fuel to the carburetor), we must make another mechanical adjustment in our carburetor (wrists and hands). We must be sure that the brain fuel will flow through freely and properly and with no restrictions.

To find out what the correct position of the wrists is at the top of the backswing, resume once again the full address position.

While holding onto the club, straighten up your back, bringing the club up with you, until you are standing straight with your arms and club extended straight out in front of you. (See p. 131.) Arms, hands, clubshaft and clubhead are at shoulder height, horizontal to the ground. Wrists, clubshaft, and arms, while extended out in front of you, should be in the same relative position they were in the address position. While your hands and clubshaft remain as they were at the address position and as they are now, they are in a position of no wrist cock or zero wrist cock.

Still keeping the arms and hands level and extended where they are now, using your hands and wrists, let the clubhead travel back and toward the right. While doing this make sure that the clubhead stays on the same level and does not dip down or rise. Make sure that the clubhead travels back on a plane level with your left arm. Let the clubhead go back as far as your wrists will allow, without opening the hands and still keeping the clubhead on this level plane. You are now in a position of full wrist cock—or 100 per cent wrist cock. The clubhead should go back level and in a line with your left arm. Wrists are now in the perfect wrist cock position for you. (See p. 132.)

You will find that in a full wrist cock the full cock will not be quite as much as expected. If a complete circle were made, using the clubhead as the periphery or outer

Proper use of wrists and hands

edge of the circle and the hands and wrists as the hub, this circle would be 360 degrees. Half of this circle would be 180 degrees. One-fourth of this circle would be 90 degrees. You will find that the average person's wrist cock will only allow the clubhead to travel to approximately 90 degrees.

There is no set rule as to how far or how many degrees a clubhead will travel in a full wrist cock. It depends upon the flexibility of the individual's wrists. The position of full or 100 per cent wrist cock may vary with each individual. Make yourself familiar with the feel and position of your hands and wrists while they are in full wrist cock, for this is something that you will have to allow to take place by itself. Practice this little wrist exercise going from zero to full wrist cock.

A good morning exercise for position would be to do this zero to 100 per cent wrist cock while holding the arms and club up at shoulder height, fifteen times each morning. In a couple of weeks you will have it down pat so that your clubhead, hands, and wrists will instinctively find the correct slot for your full wrist cock. If, on the way back in this exercise, your clubhead dips below the level of your left arm, your wrists will be in a position for hooking the ball. If your clubhead rises above the level of your left arm, you will be in a position for slicing. If the clubhead goes back properly on the same level as your left arm you will have a straight ball.

Another good way of practicing the correct left-hand

A. First step in exercise for strengthening and obtaining the proper wrist action. While in the proper hold, lift arms and clubhead at shoulder height. (Exercise 3.)

B. Without turning the body and still keeping the arms stretched out in front of you, cock the wrists so that the clubhead and shaft travel along the path in line with the left arm. Repeat this cocking and uncocking exercise so that it can be done naturally so that when the wrists relax on the way back, the clubhead will go into this proper slot of its own accord.

Proper use of wrists and hands

wrist cock is while seated at a table or desk. Place the left palm and arm, up to the elbow, flat against the surface of the table or the desk. Make a fist and without lifting it, cock the wrist back as far as it will go while still keeping the fist and knuckles touching the flat surface. (See page 34.)

This is the correct wrist cock position for you. You will notice that there will not be as much wrist cock as you thought. Practice this exercise at odd moments where it is convenient for you to do so, and the benefit you will get from it will be immeasurable.

Now try this zero to 100 per cent wrist cock with your left arm at various different heights. Try it at the address position, with the left arm half-way back, and at the top of the backswing. Familiarize yourself with the feeling of the wrists being in the correct wrist cock at the top of the backswing, not only by looking and checking the position, but better still, by sensing the correct position. The correct position should be so well learned that if you were to swing your arms back, your relaxed hands and wrists would form the wrist cock position. This wrist-cock position can be reached in two ways, and they are both correct. You can consciously cock the wrists yourself on the way back, or you can allow the momentum of the left arm to cause the relaxed wrists to cock by themselves.

Let us mentally go through the full backswing again so that you can add the correct wrist cock to the backswing.

Begin from the address position and go through from

Exercise showing how to acquire the correct wrist cock at the top of the backswing. A. Rest left palm and forearm flat on desk or table.

B. Make fist. Make sure knuckles remain in contact with table.

C. Cock wrist toward right without lifting knuckles from the table. This is the correct wrist cock for you. Strive through practice to make the wrist cock as full as possible. This little exercise can be done at odd moments during the day.

Proper use of wrists and hands

the start, the forward press, to the complete top of the backswing. After the forward press of the feet, the feet will turn the hips, the hips will carry the shoulders. After the shoulders have carried the arms part of the way back, then the left arm takes over and continues going back. At this point, as the left arm takes over and starts going back, consciously start cocking the wrists so that at the top of the backswing the arms and the clubhead will reach the full wind up at the same time. It is not wrong to consciously start cocking the wrists at any point in the back swing, so long as at the top of the back swing the wrists are fully cocked.

If you are to allow the wrists to cock by themselves, because of the momentum of the left arm, the wrists will begin to start cocking as soon as the left arm begins to near the top of its position at the top of the backswing. The arm will be in its place before the clubhead has completed its journey. You are now in a perfect position at the top of the backswing.

Once the wrists are fully cocked, whether consciously or not, then the wrists and hands have completed their work in the golf swing. They do nothing more.

13.
The wrist and hands in the downswing

LEAVING THE WRISTS AND HANDS AS THEY ARE AND doing nothing more with them from this top of the backswing position, pull down with your left arm and left hand while still keeping the left hand as it is in the full wrist cock position. Pull down and through right to the finish of your golf swing, letting the momentum created by the left arm uncock your wrists so that the clubhead will hit the ball freely and unaided by the hands. The force and energy of this pull down comes from the left arm only.

The downswing starts by the pulling down of the left arm.

As you pull down with your left arm and hand, keeping the left arm and hand in control, maintain the full extension of the left arm. Do not collapse it on the way down. In starting to pull down, do not turn your shoulders, hips, or knees until after the arm, hands and wrists, which should remain in the full cock position, are well started on the way down.

If you turn your shoulders or hips before starting down with the left arm, you will throw that arm out of its in-to-out orbit. Keep the distance from the shoulder to the wrist bone constant and, while doing this, quietly guide

FLAIL

the left arm in the correct path you expect your clubhead to take. Get the feeling that your left arm and hand are traveling from the top of the backswing down to under your right shoulder, and up over your left shoulder.

Perhaps it surprises you that the hands do nothing on the way down, and that the left arm starts down before the hips move. I shall explain. But first, let me congratulate you as you are now ready for one of the truly great secrets of the golf swing.

Fortunately, you can be quickly guided to a point of great skill by the proper understanding of the art of physical release. Before I can explain why the hands and wrists do nothing, or why you should start your downswing with the pulling down of your left arm, I must let you know that, on the way down to and through the ball from the top of the backswing to the finish of your swing, *the hands do nothing*. They merely hold onto the club handle. Contradictory? Yes, but let us find out how we arrive at this conclusion.

Many years ago, the farmers of Europe were thrashing wheat with just an ordinary plain stick. Then one farmer got an idea. He took a stick, attached a strip of leather to the end of it and then added another stick to the other end of the leather strip. He reasoned that if he hit the wheat holding onto one stick, the stick on the other end of the leather strip would smash into the wheat with much greater force and speed than he could ever create using the single stick. He would also be using only half the strength he would ordinarily with a single stick.

This action caused by the pliable strip of leather is called the flailing action. The principle of the flail is the same we use in the perfect golf swing. The left arm represents a stick. The wrists represent a strip of leather attached to the hands which are attached to the handle of the club. If the hands hold the club too tightly, you lose the flexibility of the wrists, and the principle of the flail is lost.

The hands hold the club handle without tension or thorough concentration, giving the necessary relaxation to the wrists and arms. The handle should be held with the same ease a little child holds onto your finger. He grips it firmly, yet you marvel at the strength of the tiny fist. This is because the child does not think of how to hold the finger. It just happens naturally.

By holding the handle in this manner, your wrists will retain the freedom and pliability they should have. The power that comes through this freedom is unbelievable. It is like the unlimited power of water which, in time, can overcome almost any obstacle by its gentleness and pliability.

The wrists and hands in the downswing

This pliability should be centered more in the wrists than in the hands. If the hands are tight and firm, the wrists will follow suit, and you will lose the desired flexibility. However, there are various degrees of firmness in the hands each person can use and still maintain the pliability desired in the wrists. Each person must find his own degree of looseness so that he does not lose the club and still keep his wrists in this flexible, relaxed state, so that the principle of the flail is not lost. Usually, if a person uses a tight hold on the handle the result will be rigid wrists.

One of the magical keys of great power in the golf swing is to make sure that your wrists and hands, on the way down, are free from tension and attention, so that they can respond and uncock as a result of the force created by the pulling down of the left arm.

If holding the club handle loosely insures this, then I strongly recommend it. Do not worry about the handle slipping out of your hands. You can hold on to the club without letting it go and still retain the flexibility of the hands and wrists. If the handle seems as if it wants to turn in your hands, do not fight it by gripping tighter. Merely allow your hands to turn with the clubhead.

How you get the full wrist cock position at the top of the backswing is not too important. The important thing is that, on the way down, the flexibility of the wrists is not lost. It is correct to start the clubhead by relaxing the wrists and allowing the clubhead to drag back and then allowing the momentum of the left arm to cause the club-head to cock the wrists. In this way you will have flexible wrists throughout the swing, and this is what is desired.

It is also correct to take the clubhead back without re-laxing your wrists, keeping the wrists locked, and then consciously cocking the wrists at the top of the backswing. So long as on the way down you unlock and relax the wrists so that flexibility of the wrists creates the necessary lag of the clubhead.

Let us say that a full wrist cock is 100 per cent and that no wrist cock is zero. Some top golfers go to 75 per cent wrist cock at the top of their backswing, and then, on the way down, the wrists, because of the relaxation due to great skill, continue cocking to full wrist cock posi-tion. Other top golfers may go to fifty, ninety, or even a hundred per cent wrist cock.

Most top golfers have this one thing in common. Their wrists continue cocking on the way down and, if the wrists are fully cocked at the top of the backswing the wrists, as a result of this downward pull will cock to an even greater degree.

You probably have noticed as you watched the better players swing, that they have a distinctive drop of the clubhead at the start of the downswing. This continuation of wrist cock is responsible for the action you see taking place in the skilled golf swing.

The wrists continue cocking on the way down.

Although we know that the power of the flail is tre-mendous, how can we be absolutely sure that this is the

The wrists and hands in the downswing

best manner of swinging a golf club? We have heard so much about waiting to come into the hitting area of the ball and then snapping the clubhead through with the right hand. One way that it can be quickly proven is to hit a few balls both ways and see for yourself which is the better method. Although I have given you a few examples of why the hands should not be used on the way down, let us continue our research.

Because of its great power the type of energy that we want to use in the golf swing comes from the principle of centrifugal force. The flailing action makes this principle possible and helps transmit this force to the clubhead. But there is another type of strength that can be used in hitting a golf ball. It is the strength of lever and fulcrum. Strength can be greatly increased by using a lever placed on a stone which acts as a fulcrum upon which the lever is placed, and a greater weight can be lifted in this manner than in the ordinary way.

Shall we use the power of fulcrum, or centrifugal force? There is no doubt as to the obvious answer. For there is no contest between centrifugal force and the power of the lever and fulcrum. Although the lever and the fulcrum can greatly increase the strength of the average man, the measure of the strength of the fulcrum depends upon

LEVER

← FULCRUM

the strength of the lever, and each lever has its breaking point. The power of centrifugal force, though, is unlimited, enough to keep the earth in its orbit.

In the golf swing we want moving clubhead speed through centrifugal force. If the principle of lever and fulcrum were used in the golf swing then the left hand must momentarily stop to create the fulcrum point so that the right hand can uncock and hit at the ball, and mainly only the strength of the right hand would be used in sending the clubhead to the ball. And this is not the way the greatest clubhead speed could be developed. This in itself should be enough to eliminate any doubt as to whether you should hit at the ball with your hands or allow the centrifugal force to control the movements of your hands and wrists.

But let us explore further. Let us exaggerate the length of the average shaft assuming that it is three times as long as the ordinary shaft, like a fishing pole, so that you can visualize what takes place in the shaft while you are swinging. If you hit with the right hand on the way down, the clubhead will lag back. The harder you hit, the more the club will lag; in fact, the clubhead would lag so far behind that it would be necessary for you to almost stop the swing in order for the clubhead to catch up with your hands. You could not deliver too much clubhead speed to the ball.

Actually it is the flexibility of the clubshaft that helps make up for the loss of speed resulting in right handhitting.

The wrists and hands in the downswing

And if it were not for the flexibility of the clubshaft the fellows hitting solely with the right hand would get little or no club snap into the ball. In fact, it is the flexibility of the clubshaft that makes the swing so intriguing. If the clubshaft had no whip at all there would be no problem. The ball would be hit merely by the uncocking of the hands and only the fellows with very strong arms and hands would be able to hit the ball a long way. The little fellow would have trouble as he would not be able to hit the ball out far enough to score well.

It is the flexibility of the shaft that makes the mastery of the golf swing an art. But let us assume that, regardless of what has been said, we are still going to use the right hand to flick the clubhead to the ball. What about timing? Would we be able to time accurately the exact instant when we should hit with the right hand?

If, while driving your car, you get a command from the brain to step on the brakes while going at a speed of sixty miles an hour, the automobile will travel many feet before the brain impulse or message travels to the base of your spine and thence to your feet so that your feet can respond to the brain impulse by stepping on the brakes.

A golf club in the delivery of a good golf swing travels approximately one hundred miles an hour. So if you think that you can time the exact instant you should use your right hand to flick the clubhead to the ball, in the time it takes the clubhead to travel the short distance from the top of the backswing to the ball, you are mistaken. You would have to start hitting with your right hand right from the top of the backswing in order to time the hit accurately.

However, there are many fine golfers who do swing this way and get some very good results. No one can say they are swinging incorrectly if they are satisfied with their performance. But, would he be getting the most out of his physical equipment? Emphatically *no!*

Remember the flail? The farmer could beat the wheat using only one stick but, by using the flail, he could get more force in his stroke and he would not have to work half as hard.

Of course, you can score well with almost any type of swing, as long as you are big enough to hit the ball out far enough to reach the greens with your second shot. Notice that I said if you are big enough. But, what about women and the little fellows who are not quite big enough to drive the ball a long way by snapping their hands at the ball? They would have to resort to the science of proper swinging, and the flail is the key to the open sesame of success in golf.

While I am not saying it is wrong to swing any way you like, you will get the best results by allowing the wrists and hands to act solely as a result of the movement of the arms and the centrifugal pull of the clubhead. The more freedom the wrists and hands have, as they come into the ball, the longer and straighter will the ball travel.

The topnotch golfer does a great deal of practicing. He hits golf balls almost every day. This hitting of balls every-

The wrists and hands in the downswing

day builds in him a tremendous amount of confidence. Confidence, in turn, gives relaxation. It is the relaxation that causes the wrists to unhinge freely and allows centrifugal force to take over, giving·you the flailing action. And it is this force that causes you to see the wrists uncocking as they come through to the ball, giving you the impression that it is the hands that are doing the uncocking. Although the seasoned golfer may sincerely feel he is using his right hand to deliver the clubhead to the ball, *the major force responsible for the uncocking of the wrists is centrifugal force.*

It is like learning to write. When you first start you grip the pencil very tightly, with poor results. As you improve, you begin loosening the grip on the pencil and the writing becomes smoother.

Through movies and with the help of photographs, there have been some very capable and excellent descriptions of what movements take place in the golf swing; but unfortunately, the description of what muscular execution takes place in an act, and the performance of the act, are two entirely different fields.

It is like the tightrope walker who describes how and where he will place his feet on the wire when walking across Niagara. Describing it and doing it are worlds apart. Many people do not understand this and are constantly looking for a mechanical order of movements which will enable them to hit the ball straight and far.

This order of muscular movements cannot be found.

The wrists and hands in the downswing

First, the perfect description of what takes place, or the perfect description of anything, even of the smallest particle of dust, would take an everlasting time. Secondly, let us assume that you do have a complete list of the order of the mechanical muscular movements that take place in a golf swing; and you follow this order of movements to the letter. No matter how well you follow this order, your best result would only be an imitation of the real thing.

The true achievement of art is the concealment of art. Art becomes perfection when it is no longer art.

In the beginning it is necessary to go through the preliminary stages of physical learning just as the artist did with the clay on the golf statue. He first created the correct basic foundation. He then built the statue in an abstract manner so that the final details could eventually be brought out. And so it is with the golf swing. It should be learned in an abstract manner. Get the major parts of the body working correctly, and the details will take care of themselves.

If we were to check again with the aid of a slow-motion camera to see what starts first in the downswing, we would find that with most top-notch golfers the hips do usually start moving first, and it is a correct interpretation of the start of the downswing. But, let us not forget that these top golfers are in the highest bracket of physical skill and if you are in the 80, and above, bracket and try to imitate the top golfers, the results will be inadequate.

The wrists and hands in the downswing

Remember the four swings of golf and the different brackets of skill? See page 84 if you need a refresher.

Now is the time when you will benefit most from your knowledge that there are these four mental and physical interpretations of swing execution.

Because the downswing is the part of the swing where the correct level of execution will be most telling, what we have done up to this point has prepared the body to accept any degree of force or level of skill.

It would be practically impossible to break the 100 bracket without a correct address position and a correct finish position, regardless of the manner of your downswing. By correcting the heart of your swing and establishing the centripetal point by placing your right leg at the correct angle, it will be possible for you to break the 90 bracket.

The correct position of the body from the waist up and the proper functioning of the hands and wrists will make it possible for you to break the 80 barrier.

The actual downswing and the mental interpretation of the downswing should be the same for the first three brackets of skill (from over 100 to under 80). Starting the downswing by pulling down the left arm will give you enough force and skill to shoot a very fine game of golf.

Starting down with the left arm will not change the order of movements of the downswing. It will keep your swing from becoming disconnected, as you are not quite ready and skilled enough and if you are in the under 100 bracket or just under to start with any other part of the

The wrists and hands in the downswing

body. When you have enough skill and start breaking 80 with regularity then, and only then, can you consciously direct the attention of the start of the downswing away from your left arm.

While you are starting the downswing by pulling down with your left arm, the hips will still go ahead although it may feel as if your arm were moving first.

The mental impression of how to start the downswing of a golfer trying to go from 100 to the high 70's is entirely different than the mental impression of the start of the downswing by a golfer shooting par or better.

The hips do start first in the downswing. Actually, it is almost impossible to start the downswing without the hips moving first. If you were to throw a ball overhand you would find that the hips would move first naturally. So why teach a movement that occurs instinctively?

But, unless you are in the highest bracket of skill, the body will be of very little help to the left arm. To prove this, take your golf club in both hands and with the club-shaft make believe that you are trying to saw down a tree at a height above the waist. In going through this sawing motion, you will notice that the hips will move first by themselves as you are sawing with your arms and hands. Then, relax your arms and hands and see if you can saw the tree by just using your hips. It cannot be done. By using the hips you are breaking the connection of your arms to your body. So, until you get the knack of it and are

The wrists and hands in the downswing

under the 80 bracket with regularity, you should start your downswing by pulling down the left arm.

In doing this, try to keep the left arm at its full extension. While keeping the arm at full extension, get the feeling that the energy of this left arm pull-down is centered in the area of your left wrist bone, thereby getting the attention away from the wrists and hands. This will keep them relaxed and fully cocked on the way down to the ball. Another way of keeping the wrists fully cocked, as you come into the ball, is to get the impression that you are trying to hit or stab the ball with the top of the handle of the club. In doing this you may feel the club lagging way back. This is correct, for only by keeping the wrists fully cocked will the clubhead lag back far enough to enable the energy of centrifugal force to take over, and cause the clubhead to smash through the ball at such a tremendous rate of speed.

Practice and play with this swing until you can execute it each time you step up to a ball, and you will be pleasantly surprised that in an amazingly short period of time you will be playing quite well. If at times you do drift off a bit, immediately check and correct your address position. Go back to the heart of your swing, the position of your right leg at the top of the backswing, and check this for correctness. If this is correct, continue checking the body from the waist up. Then check the position of your left arm at the top of the backswing. And, if this is

A. In swinging, the impression should be that you are trying to drive the *handle* of the clubshaft into, through, and past the ball. In doing this the clubhead will take over by itself without the help of the hands, wrists or body.

B. At this point the tendency to flick the clubhead is great. Here is where you must continue on past the ball. You may say, "How will the clubhead hit the ball?" Trust it and the force created by the left arm will result in the true release of centrifugal energy giving the clubhead a speed unobtainable in any other manner.

C. The mental impression should be that you are swinging far beyond the point of contact. Actually this will not be so, but this is what you should try to do in your swing.

The wrists and hands in the downswing

correct, and you are starting the downswing by the pulling down of the left arm, and if you are starting the downswing properly, then the trouble is in your hands and wrists.

The fault is that you are using your hands and wrists excessively. Relax the hands and wrists and do nothing with them on the way down and the shots will start going straight and far once again. If you do go off, the trouble will rarely be in the body; for once the body learns its basic bulk positions, it seldom goes off. The trouble will usually be in your hands. You are most likely snapping at the ball.

Another quick way to check your golf swing for correctness is by standing so that you can see the shadow of your swing on the ground or a wall. Then take a few swings and the shadow will show the abstract of the golf swing and you will quickly be able to see the over-all picture. It will then become a simple matter to make the necessary corrections to your swing.

After perfecting this swing you should be very well pleased with the results. This swing and bracket of skill should be satisfactory for the majority of golfers. By using this swing, your score can easily drop to the middle 70's and occasionally into the low 70's.

The proper way to practice-swing to learn the part the wrists, hands and arms play during the downswing. A. From this position, start down with the left forearm in command and leaving the wrists fully cocked, for once the wrists and hands are in this full wrist cock position the conscious work of the hands and wrists is over, and from then on centrifugal energy takes over and is responsible for the uncocking of the wrists and the unleashing of tremendous clubhead speed through the ball. (Exercise 5.)

B. Pull down with left arm to a point approximately waist high without moving the body. This should be the manner of starting the downswing for anyone striving to go from over a 100 to under 80.

C. Continue down and past the ball with the wrists still fully cocked. The body will now have moved to compliment the movement of the arms. *Do not uncock wrists.*

D. Continue on past the ball with the wrists still fully cocked.

E. Body will have completed its turn and arms still continue
upward with wrists still fully cocked.

F. Continue arms to completion of swing still keeping wrists
fully cocked. Club shaft will be lifted over head.

G. Arms continue toward final resting place. Wrists are still fully cocked.

H. Finish of exercise. Arms have completed the full swing. Wrists have remained fully cocked. Note: This is the mental impression you should have of your golf swing. When done at a greater speed, it will be impossible to hold the wrists cocked as the centrifugal force will force the wrists to uncock. At a tremendous rate of speed, if any attention or activity is given to your wrists and hands during the downswing, this attention and usage will prevent true centrifugal force from taking over. The result will be a great loss of speed and accuracy. When you are extremely skillful, the relaxation of the wrists and hands during the downswing will cause centrifugal force instinctively to take over. The result will be a straight and very long ball.

14.
The ultimate
golf swing

IF YOU ARE A PERFECTIONIST AND ARE CONTENT only with the best, or are aspiring to greatness in golf, then the next and final bracket of skill should be entered. But I must give you a word of warning. If you are not truly prepared for this high level of skill it will do you little good. Make sure, before attempting to penetrate this final and highest bracket of skill, that you have played in the aforementioned manner for a while and are doing quite well at it; for then, and only then, should you attempt the execution of the ultimate and most powerful swing—the swing that will make it possible for you to reach your pinnacle of golf; a level of skill so high that it acts by itself. For, this is the only true natural way of action, as when the eyes see or the ears hear; each working independently and by themselves, without the necessity of being forced.

You are now penetrating a level of understanding that is so far advanced it is rarely recognized and seldom understood; and, if recognized, is very rarely explained properly.

Remember the farmer with the flail and how he took one stick and added a strip of pliable leather to the end of it; then took another stick and added it to the free end of the strip of leather?

These two sticks attached together with the strip of pliable leather gave the farmer a powerful flailing action when he beat the wheat. Remember how we used the left arm as a stick and the wrists and hands as a strip of leather attached to the shaft? Remember the tremendous whip that could be created with the clubhead by doing nothing with the hands and wrists but by just letting them remain free, pliable and responsive to the action of the left arm?

In the ultimate golf swing—the swing that invades and breaks the highest bracket of skill—not only must the wrists and hands be pliable like the strip of leather but the shoulders and left arm must also be transformed into a piece of pliable leather. In fact, everything from the waist up must be transformed into a pliable and lifeless piece of leather.

Everything from the feet to the hips represents one stick. Everything from the hips to the clubhandle represents a piece of pliable leather attached to the clubhandle. Now you have the most powerful human flail possible.

The ultimate golf swing

You do nothing consciously from the waist up. Everything that happens from there should be a result of the movements of the feet, legs and hips. All movements from the waist up take place as a result of the movements of the hips. The hips are controlled by the feet and legs which are in command and are the controlling factor of your swing in regard to movement and power.

The feet being in direct contact with the earth create the base of the foundation through which a tremendous amount of energy can be delivered to the ball. This great power comes mainly from the feet. The feet get their strength from the earth. The closer to the feet you call upon for the source of energy and strength, the greater the power delivered to the ball.

As in Greek mythology when Hercules fought the giant Antaeus, each time Antaeus was thrown to the ground, he got up with greater and renewed strength. Antaeus received his strength from the earth. Hercules, upon learning this, lifted Antaeus above his head so that the feet of Antaeus could not touch the earth and thereby deprived him of renewed strength. You could not hit a ball too far if you were suspended in air.

And so it is in the golf swing; the closer to the soles of the feet the main source of energy is derived, the greater the power delivered to the ball. The whole concept of the golf swing now begins to change. On the way back the feet and legs turn the hips. The left hip turns the relaxed shoulders. The shoulders fling the arms back into the proper position.

The left arm, while being flung back by the shoulders, if relaxed, will maintain its full extension during the swing as the result of the pulling force of the clubhead upon the relaxed left arm. The extension must be maintained in a very quiet and unstrained manner as in the pointing of your finger. It must be maintained at its full length by a visualization of the fullest possible radius that the left arm and hand can create.

Once at the top of the backswing, the mechanical and mental interpretation of the downswing changes. The attention which was centered on the left arm pulling down at the start now shifts way down to the feet. The downswing of the ideal golf swing starts with the feet. The feet activate the legs and the legs turn the hips. The left hip is directly connected to the clubhead and, as the left hip goes through, the left hip pulls the clubhead to and through the ball. It should feel as though everything from the left hip to the ball is blank and that nothing exists from the waist up except this direct connection of the left hip to the clubhead.

The clubhead will take the same path through the ball that the left hip takes. The right hip helps the left hip pull through by pushing the left hip along the path that the left hip is guiding the clubhead in. If you mentally guide the left hip along the inside-out path, the clubhead will follow along this correct clubpath, and the result will be a straight, long ball. The path of the clubhead is directly controlled by the left hip.

If the left hip guides the clubhead a little sharper from the inside-out path, a hook will be the result. If a slice or fade is desired, let the left hip cut across the ball the desired amount and the clubhead will follow the path of the left hip and you will get your slice or fade. As you become more skillful just the visualization of the type of shot needed will cause the hip to take the desired path resulting in the desired trajectory.

There must be no conscious effort to guide or hit the ball with the hands, arms, shoulders, back or stomach. All the work must be done with the feet which, with the help of the legs, will activate the hips and allow the left hip to take over as it is in direct contact with the clubhead. The hips do not supply the power. They merely act as the distributors of the great energy coming from the feet.

As your feet cause the hips to turn in the downswing, there must be enough relaxation in the area of the waist so as to allow the shoulders to lag back. The more freedom in the area of the waist, the more evident will be the principle of the body flail and the more power you will get.

The more you try to help the swing by hitting with the shoulders, back, stomach, arms or hands, the more you rob the body of the desirable flexibility that it should have and transform it into a solid firmness with no pliability or speed. The more muscle and strength you use in your golf swing, the more you tend to slow up the clubhead.

The muscles of the body act in a very peculiar way. If you were to bend your arm fully, what takes place is this: The biceps contract, bending the arm. If you were to then straighten your arm, the biceps would not stretch and straighten the arm. The biceps would relax and the muscle in the back of your arm, the triceps, would contract, straightening the arm. Upon usage, the muscles contract, tighten up, and act as brakes that hold.

Any attention you give to any part of your body will tend to activate the muscles in that area, thereby tightening and destroying your relaxation. Your attention must be completely away from your body. Even though the positions that you think of may be correct, the fact that you are thinking of them is detrimental to skill.

It is like trying to tell a little boy of nine years of age not to be afraid of the dark and explaining to him that there is no reason to be afraid. Then you give him many good and logical explanations as to why he should not be afraid. The more reasons you give, the more fear you instill.

But, before you can stop thinking of physical execution, you must first sever your teacher-pupil relations with your

The ultimate golf swing

teacher. Unfortunately, there are some teachers instructing in many fields of physical endeavor who are actually preventing their pupils from ever attaining the great skill that is possible in the pupil by the continuance of instruction. Actually, the teacher is acting as a crutch to the pupil.

When the pupil, for whatever the reason, breaks away from the teacher, and finally says, "I'm going to do this in my own way," then and only then will he begin to show the naturalness and great skill with which he may be gifted. This severance, this drifting apart of teacher and pupil, must come about in order for the pupil to reach his latent possibilities for proficiency. How this severance of teacher and pupil comes about is of little importance. It can be done by the pupil, or it can come about by the intelligent and unselfish sacrifice of the teacher. Then and only then has the teacher truly completed his work and done a thorough job of teaching.

When you finally feel that the method you employ is your very own, only then can you begin to direct your attention away from yourself.

And as you become more and more skillful, the mental picture of the action of your feet and legs will gradually vanish. It will be only the left hip hitting the ball and when you become a truly fine player, even the thought of your hips hitting the ball will eventually leave you.

The ultimate golf swing

As soon as you start hitting a few good shots, do not become overconfident as this will excite you, and you will lose the good beginning. Neither should you show the least emotion over a missed shot. Just learn to accept the good and bad shots as they come and your performance will improve by leaps and bounds.

The more attention given to your swing, the lower the degree of skill. Strive to completely erase from your mind the mechanical execution of the shot and concentrate on the end result, the place where the ball will come to rest. If, while concentrating, an interfering thought jumps into your mind, do not fight it in an attempt to *retain* your proper concentration. Simply push it aside very casually as you would push a twig out of your way while walking through the brushes.

When you are performing at this high pitch of skill, if your attention is distracted or brought to any part of your body, whether it is a good or bad suggestion, unless you quietly put the interfering thought aside and ignore it, the result will be a deterioration of skill. Anything that brings your attention to position or order of movement will destroy your skill. Emotions can do this also—the desire to do well, fear of making a mistake, checking to make sure everything is in its proper position, ego—all of these emotions tend to destroy skill. The mind should be far away from your body and the execution of movement.

The ultimate golf swing

In swinging, you should feel that your arms, hands and shoulders do not belong to you, that they do not exist, and that you have no control over the clubhead.

You should feel as though it is only the left hip and the clubhead that are involved in the swinging of your club and eventually, even the thought of the hips and clubhead will vanish and your attention will start going completely away from yourself, and focusing on where you want the ball to end up. Only then will you experience the thrill of true physical excellence.

Swinging in this manner, with the power and energy of your swing coming from your feet, will enable you to take any club and hit the ball not only the full length that the club will give you, but also half, three-quarters or even one-quarter of the full length. You do not regulate the length of your shot by a mechanical adjustment of your body but by a mental command that you want the ball to end up at a certain distance.

It's just like throwing a baseball. You do not measure the length of your backswing for the particular distance you want to throw the ball. You merely look and throw, and the supply of energy takes care of itself. By just the visualization of the length needed in a golf shot, your feet will instinctively supply you with the necessary power to reach your target.

If you want to walk faster, you do not say, "I am going

to move my feet faster." You just think of how fast you
want to walk and the legs and feet act by themselves.

In order to get your maximum length, you must think
far to hit far.

Herein lies the secret of ultimate skill in physical endeavor. The true achievement of art is the concealment
of art. And so it is in the golf swing; if it acts, it must act
by itself without mental or physical interference.

The best instruction is no instruction.

I DO NOT TEACH — I SIMPLY

SEEK THE TRUTH.

Socrates

15.
Golf exercises

HERE IS A QUICK SUMMARY OF THE LITTLE EXER-
cises that can be done at home in your leisure time. Not
only will they help your golf swing but they will also help
keep you in good physical condition.

These simple exercises should take only a few minutes
of your time to perform and the resulting good health and
better golf will definitely warrant the expenditure of time
spent.

	Benefit—Golf	*Benefit—Health*
Exercise #1 Ten Times. (See p. 65)	Follow-through.	Balance and flexibility of the spinal cord.
Exercise #2 Ten Times. (See p. 90 and p. 106)	Touching wall, correct right leg and trunk posi- tion at top of backswing.	Stretching back and arm muscles. Toning the muscles in area of your back.

	Benefit—Golf	*Benefit—Health*
Exercise #3 Ten Times. Exercise #4	Correct wrist cock and aiding flexibility of the wrists.	Strengthening of the area of the muscles of the arms, shoulders and stomach.
Exercise #5 Five Times. (See p. 154)	Slow motion swing without wrist cock, gives you correct mental picture of the golf swing.	Over-all body toning up.
Exercise #6 (See p. 174)	Sharpening your eyesight.	

Golf exercises

This exercise is also discussed in my book on putting and chipping.

Because good eyesight is important in improving your golf game, some simple eye exercises might prove beneficial in developing your master eye and your depth eye, as well as improving your right angle vision. Let it be understood that I am making no claims to having developed these systems. Nor do I claim that you can throw away your glasses after using these routines. However, these exercises have been advised and suggested by qualified ophthalmologists to help improve vision and especially to relieve eye strain.

Eye Exercises

No. 1 Without moving your head, focus your eyes on the top right-hand corner of your room. Then shift your gaze, without moving your head, to the bottom lefthand corner, diagonally across the room. Shift your gaze from the upper right to the lower left, back and forth, ten times. Then do the shifting exercises for the other corners, from upper left to lower right, in a similar manner. Repeat until you have focused on each corner ten times.

No. 2 As in Exercise No. 1, without moving your head move your eyes slowly from side to side, from the extreme left to the extreme right, along a horizontal plane. Repeat these motions ten times.

Golf exercises

No. 3   Once more, without moving your head, first focus your eyes up and then focus them as far down as possible. Repeat this exercise ten times.

No. 4   Roll your eyes to the left, in a clockwise direction, making a complete revolution of the eyes. Do this for ten repetitions. Reverse the motion, rolling your eyes in a counter-clockwise direction, through a complete revolution. Repeat ten times.

No. 5   Extend your hand, palm towards you, at arm's length. Now focus your eyes on the palm. Shift your gaze to a distant object—perhaps a light fixture on the ceiling or some similar object. Alternate focusing on the palm and on the distant object at least ten times, spending a few seconds on each object.

No. 6   Imagine that a mosquito is crawling across the ceiling or wall. Remembering that the path of this insect may be erratic—sometimes fast, sometimes slow, never in a straight line—follow the imaginary trip with your eyes. Then go back to the starting point of the journey and repeat for a total of three trips.

No. 7   Blink your eyes fifty times, with your hands placed over your eyes to eliminate the entry of any possible light.

You will notice after only one session of these exercises that you are able to use your eyes with a greater degree

Golf exercises

of accuracy on the golf course. Try to develop the habit of doing these exercises once a week all year around, and you will enjoy much better vision and a pleasant improvement in your game.

BOOK II

SECRETS OF ACCURATE PUTTING AND CHIPPING

Importance of Putting

ON A PAR 72 GOLF course a perfect round of golf normally consists of fifteen tee shots with the driver, three iron shots from the tee on par 3 holes, three shots with woods in the fairway for the long par 5 holes, fifteen iron shots to the green, and thirty-six putts. Of seventy-two strokes, thirty-six, or 50 per cent, are putts. Thus, it is obvious that putting is far and away the most important part of the game; and it is here that you can really bring down your score. More tournaments are won or lost because of putting than because of any other part of the game. You can recover from a missed drive or a missed iron shot; but in shooting par you cannot recover the lost putt that should have been sunk.

Keys to a system

GREAT PUTTERS are not born; they are made. Good putting is a matter, not just of practice, but of practice with a system. In building a system there are several key points to understand.

(1) Which is your "master eye"?
(2) What is central fixation?
(3) Is your right-angle vision accurate?
(4) How can you sharpen your eyesight?
(5) What makes the ball spin properly?
(6) Where is the "sweet spot" on your putter?

(7) What type of putter should you use?

(8) What stance will give you the most consistent success?

(9) What is the proper grip and why?

(10) Where does the energy to stroke the ball come from?

(11) How can you judge distances accurately.

(12) What is the proper way to read a green.

The Master Eye

THE FIRST STEP IN building your system is to discover which is you *master eye.* Knowing which is your master eye will enable you to line up a putt with greater accuracy.

Select an object in the room, something fairly small, about the size of an ashtray or a pack of cigarettes. Then stand about fifteen feet away from the object. With both eyes open, point at the object with your right forefinger. With your finger on the target, close one eye and then the other, and you will notice your finger jumping. The eye that lines up the finger closer to the object is your master eye.

In most cases, a right-handed person's master eye is his right and a left-handed person's master eye is his left.

The eye that keeps your finger on the target is your master eye. It is the master eye, in a human being, which enables his brain to control the muscles that drive a car in a straight line, move his legs in a desired direction, and so forth. It is the master eye that gives the accurate alignment for all acts in which proper direction is needed. Therefore, in lining up your putt to the hole, stand in back of the hole so that you are forming a straight line from your master eye through the ball and to the hole. Line up your putt with your master eye.

179

Central Fixation

WHILE YOUR master eye determines direction, your other eye determines depth or distance. The point where they meet is called the point of *central fixation.** When you look at a photograph or a store window, your brain sees only one image — and that image is clearest only at the point of central fixation.

In order to see the picture or object (that is, the green or the flag or the cup) more clearly, you should blink your eyes a few times. Then focus them on various sections of the object you are looking at. In this way your brain receives more mental pictures and your vision becomes clearer. As a result, you will be able to see clearly details that you could not see before. On the green you will be able to see even the slightest slopes and undulations.

When lining up your putt, blink a few times, then focus your eyes on a few spots between the ball and the hole. You will then notice how much clearer the correct line appears.

When striving for direction, favor your master eye; when distance is paramount, favor your depth eye.

Blinking is one of nature's best eye exercises. It is especially good for relieving eye strain. (Incidentally, if you do any rifle shooting at a still target, use only your master eye. But, if you shoot at a moving target, use both eyes.)

This takes care of the forward vision. Now let's get down to the right-angle vision.

* *see illustration on following page*

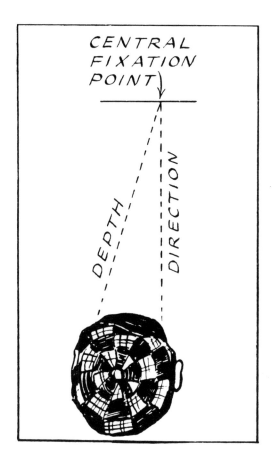

Note that the master eye has a direct line of vision, while the depth eye looks off at an angle which meets at the focal point or point of central fixation.

Right-Angle Vision

LET'S GIVE OUR EYES the "right-angle" test. This is one of the most difficult of all tasks for the human eye. Most people are off slightly to the right or to the left of their target. Only in rare cases do people have perfect right-angle alignment.

So let us find out how close you are to the correct rightangle vision. Draw a line approximately one yard long on the floor. Then take your putter and place it with the toe of the club at what you think is a perfect right angle to the line Now, without moving the putter, take a square and place it along the line, snuggling it up to the face of the putter. (See photos on the following pages.) This shows you immediately whether you are in proper alignment. If not, you can tell in which direction you are off. You can then aim to the right or the left of your target, as the case may be, compensating for the degree to which you are off.

Do not worry about not being able to place your putter at a perfect right angle. It is normal not to be able to do so. Most people are off either to the right or to the left. *The trick is to find out in which direction you are off and to allow for this in your putting.*

There is a great feeling of confidence in knowing that your putter blade is in proper alignment with the hole. It makes for increased relaxation so that you can stroke your ball with greater smoothness and confidence.

The square, when placed on the line and almost touching the putter blade, clearly shows whether your blade is at a right angle to the intended line.

184

Sharpening Your Eyesight

BECAUSE GOOD eyesight is important in improving your golf game, some simple eye exercises might prove beneficial in developing your master eye and your depth eye, as well as in improving your right-angle vision. Let it be understood that I am making no claims to having developed these systems. Nor do I claim that you can throw away your glasses after using these routines. However, these exercises have been advised and suggested by qualified ophthalmologists to help improve vision and especially to relieve eye strain.

The first four exercises are best done just before you fall asleep; while you can do exercises five, six, and seven at odd moments during the day.

Exercise 1

WITHOUT MOVING your head, focus your eyes on the top right-hand corner of your room. Then shift your gaze, without moving your head, to the bottom left-hand corner, diagonally across the room. Shift your gaze from the upper right to the lower left, back and forth, ten times. Then do the shifting exercises for the other corners, from upper left to lower right, in a similar manner. Repeat the exercise until you have focused on each corner ten times.

Exercise 2

AS IN EXERCISE ONE, without moving your head, move your eyes slowly from side to side, from the extreme left to the extreme right, along a horizontal plane. Repeat these motions ten times.

Exercise 3

ONCE MORE, without moving your head, first focus your eyes up and then focus them as far down as possible. Repeat this exercise ten times.

Exercise 4

ROLL YOUR EYES to the left, in a clockwise direction, making a complete revolution of the eyes. Do this for ten repetitions.

Reverse the motion, rolling your eyes in a counterclockwise direction through a complete revolution. Repeat ten times.

Exercise 5

EXTEND YOUR HAND, palm towards you, at arm's length. Now focus you eyes on the palm. Shift your gaze to a distant object — perhaps a light fixture on the ceiling or some similar object. Alternate focusing on the palm and on the distant object at least ten times, spending a few seconds on each object.

Exercise 6

IMAGINE that a mosquito is crawling across the ceiling or wall. Remembering that the path of this insect may be erratic—sometimes fast, sometimes slow, almost never in a straight line—follow the imaginary trip with your eyes. Then go back to the starting point of the journey and repeat for a total of three trips.

Exercise 7

BLINK YOUR EYES fifty times, with your hands placed over your eyes to eliminate the entry of any possible light.

YOU WILL NOTICE after only one session of these exercises that you are able to use your eyes with a greater degree of accuracy on the golf course. Try to develop the habit of doing these exercises once a week all year around, and you will enjoy much better vision and a pleasant improvement in your game.

Proper Spin of the Ball

THE OBJECT IN putting is to sink the ball as often as you possibly can. In order to do this, you must give the ball the proper spin. If you strike across the ball from left to right (as in sketch A on page 188), causing it to spin from left to right, it will go true only until it starts to slow down. Then it will curve from left to right. On the other hand, if you strike the ball from right to left (as in sketch B), again it will go true only until the major part of its force is spent. Then it will curve to the left in the same direction of the spin, causing a miss.

In order to keep the ball on line, it must be stroked in a straight line, causing the ball to overspin and thereby eliminating any tendency to curve. Overspin actually causes the ball to hug the green. It is a known fact that a rolling ball will always have overspin. The gravitational pull on a rolling sphere will keep the bottom of the sphere hugging the earth while the top keeps rolling over.

Now, in putts that are stroked across the intended line of flight, you will also have overspin. It is the additional sidespin caused from the cut stroke that causes the ball to curve near the end of its journey, causing you to miss hole. So, if you can stroke the ball in a manner free from any tendency toward sidespin, you have the perfect stroke. This same principle applies in billiards, ping-pong, and tennis.

With the correct overspin, although you may stroke the ball hard enough to go a few feet past the hole, the overspin will tend to curve the ball downward so as to sink the ball if it just touches the lip of the cup.

In order to get the desired overspin, the ball must be played far enough forward so that the ball will be struck after the club passes the bottom of its arc and is on its way up (as in sketch C). That is why we play the ball exactly off the left toe.

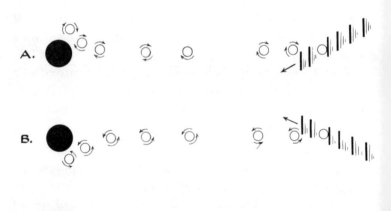

Effect on ball as clubhead strikes ball in the different paths.

OVERSPIN ON A TENNIS BALL

Overspin on tennis ball caused ball to drop sharply.

SPIN OF THE BALL

OVERSPIN ON A PING-PONG BALL

Sharp drop on ping-pong ball is also caused by the spin applied.

OVERSPIN ON A GOLF BALL
WITH THE CORRECT PUTTING STROKE

Notice that the stroke is rising after contact with ball, thereby eliminating any tendency toward sidespin.

The "Sweet Spot" on Your Putter

ON WHAT PART OF the putter should the ball be struck?" is a question that has bothered quite a few golfers.

Every putter has a "sweet spot." You should discover this spot on your putter. Hold your putter between the thumb and forefinger of your left hand. Then take a coin and tap it along the face of your putter. When you can tap the coin and feel no vibration in the fingers holding the club, you have found the "sweet spot." It is this spot that should come in contact with the ball when the ball is struck.

You will find that the "sweet spot" is usually slightly behind the center of your blade. This is the point of the least amount of turn in the putting blade. If you turn your putter blade quickly from left to right, opening and closing the face of the blade, you will notice that the sweet spot on your putter is doing the least amount of turning.

In stroking your putt, see to it that the ball is met in the sweet spot. You will give yourself a better chance for more sinks. Now let's go on to the selection of your putter.

SIDE VIEW

SWEETSPOT
BACK OF CENTER

SWEETSPOT
BACK OF CENTER

(O)

BIRD'S-EYE VIEW

SQUARE   CLOSED   OPEN

This clearly shows the effect of opening and closing the putter blade.

193

Tap a coin along face of putter until you reach a spot where you feel no vibration in the thumb and forefinger of the hand holding the club. That spot is the "sweet spot."

Choice of Putters

THERE ARE MANY varieties of putters on the market today and all are good putters and, when used properly, are able to send the ball into the hole repeatedly.

What should you look for in a putter? There are six vitally important features of your putter that you should consider with extreme care: (1) length, (2) weight, (3) shaft, (4) grip,(5) shape of the head, and (6) placement of the shaft in the head. Let's take them in order.

The proper length

TO FIND the proper length you need in your putter, stand with your back up against the wall. Stretch your left hand and arm at shoulder height, with the back of your hand flush against the wall. The distance from the tip of the fingers of your left hand to the middle of your chin designates the length of the putter suitable for you.

Weight of putter

THE WEIGHT of your putter should be between fifteen and eighteen ounces. The closer to fifteen ounces your putter comes, the better it will feel, since a lighter putter will give you a more delicate touch.

Shaft of putter

THE SHAFT should not be too stiff but should be pliable enough to give you the necessary clubhead "feel."

Grip on your putter

THE GRIP on your putter should have a flat front, so that you not only can see that you are holding your putter straight, but also can feel with your fingers that it is straight.

Shape of the head

NOW WE COME to the most important feature of your putter: the shape of its head. There are many sizes and shapes that are popular today. Let's find out which one will give you the greatest advantage.

What do you want your putter to be? You want it to be a tool that will give you a sensitive feel. In addition, you want it to have a head that you can place at a perfect right angle the greatest number of times.

An ideal putter is one similar to the putter diagrammed on page 193. When looking down on such a putter, you can definitely see a right angle, since the top, face, back, and toe are square. This eliminates the necessity of your lining up with just the club face, which has so little loft that it is almost impossible to see a right angle.

Of course, there have been many great players who have used differently shaped putters. But why not make it easier for your eyes by selecting a putter that is perfectly square. It will be much easier to place such a putter at a right angle to your intended line of flight.

Your putter must also have a bottom that is rounded out so as not to stick on the grass of the green when you are stroking the putt.

Placement of shaft in the head

WHERE SHOULD the shaft be in the putter head, center or back? You will find, by opening and closing the putter face, that the farther away you get from the heel of the putter, the greater degree of error.

The shaft should be placed between the heel and center of the clubhead so as not to lose the very importanat clubhead feel. This, in turn, will bring the "sweet spot" closer to the shaft, thereby minimizing the possibility of error to such a degree that, although your blade may not be at perfect right angle to your line of flight, you will still be able to sink that extra putt.

Do not imagine that it is the putter alone that will enable you to keep sinking putts. A person who is a good putter will sink putts with any kind of putter; but precision tools offer a better advantage. A piece of cloth can be cut with a pocket knife; but it can be cut much more easily with a pair of scissors.

Putting Stance

THERE IS NOTHING mysterious or complicated about building a proper putting stance. It is simply a matter of placing your feet and body in the proper position in relation to the ball and target.

In order to build a proper putting stance you need a target. Let's not use a putting cup. Let's use a very difficult target: an ordinary straight pin, stuck through a small piece of paper so that it can be seen from a distance. Now place your ball approximately six feet from the target. (Do not worry about your putting grip; we will get to that a little later on.)

Using your master eye, form an imaginary line from the pin through the center of the ball. Then place the toe of your putter in back of the ball, cutting the ball in half at a perfect right angle to the imaginary line (as in the first picture in this chapter). This will give you a finer line to work with, rather than one the thickness of the diameter of the ball.

By aiming with the toe of the putter you can also see how far away your left toe should be from the ball. Place your left foot so that your left toe is behind the ball at a perfect right angle to the imaginary line and close enough so that your eyes are directly over the ball.

Place your right foot parallel to your left. Both toes and heels should be parallel and far enough apart so that the outer edge of your feet are the same distance apart as the width of your hips.

Bend both knees slightly and equally, so that you are in a squatting position. Bending your knees will relieve nerve

SIDE VIEW

SWEETSPOT
BACK OF CENTER

SWEETSPOT
BACK OF CENTER

BIRD'S-EYE VIEW

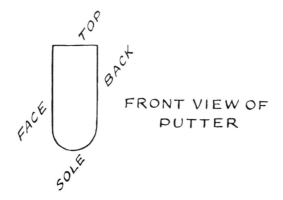

TOP

BACK

FACE

SOLE

FRONT VIEW OF
PUTTER

The toe of the putter is used as the aiming point. Ball is close enough to left toe to enable you to keep your eyes directly over ball and weight back on heels.

The toes are parallel with the intended line of flight. Eyes are directly over the ball. The right forearm is resting lightly against the right thigh and the left elbow is pointing in line with the toes. Body weight is slightly back and toward the left foot.

201

The ball is played off the left toe to allow clubface to meet the ball as the club is rising, creating the desired overspin.

Club is now in position, ready to stroke the ball with the "sweet spot," which is directly behind the center of the ball.

As it would appear to a left-handed player.

The correct putting stance. Feet are parallel to the intended
line of flight—knees slightly bent to eliminate tension. Body
weight on left foot and back toward left heel. Right arm
resting lightly on right thigh. Left elbow pointing along line
of toes. Eyes directly over ball. During actual stroking,
breath is held.

205

tension. The weight of your body should be on the left foot and toward the heels. This weight position will reduce body motion to a minimum. If your weight is equally divided, your heartbeat will make your body move. That is why the expert rifleman keeps his weight wholly on one foot. Keep yours on your left foot.

Hold your breath during the putting stroke. This will further eliminate body vibration. Of course, don't forget to resume breathing after you finish the stroke.

The distance of the ball from the left toe depends on the type of build you have. Your eyes should look down at the ball in a perfectly straight line. That will bring the ball approximately four inches away from your left toe. Very rarely is it ever farther than five inches away.

Remember, overspin is desirable. By placing the ball off the toe of your left foot, you automatically get the desired overspin. The club will be stroking the ball on the upswing, rather than on the downswing.

Just before stroking the ball, pick your putter blade off the ground very slightly and slide it forward gently and carefully while the blade is still in the air. Slide it forward until the "sweet spot" on your putter is directly in back of the ball. Do not train yourself to slide the blade forward while it is resting on the ground; for, when you are on the green, the grass will make the clubhead stick. This sliding forward will eliminate the nervous tension that is caused by jumping the blade back and forth over the ball as you address it.

Now, let's get to the all-important putting grip so that we can continue to that magic basic putting stroke.

Putting Grip

HOLD THE CLUB with the left hand only, as shown in the first picture in this chapter. Place your left thumb straight down the top of the handle of your putter. If your putter has a round handle, imagine that it is square and place your left thumb on the top of the imaginary square.

If you have long fingers, your putter handle will naturally be in your fingers. If you have short fingers, it will naturally be in your palm. There is no set rule for this, inasmuch as no two hands are built exactly alike. The important part is that your left thumb is on the top of the handle.

While holding the club just in the left hand, you will notice that your left elbow is close to your body. In this position you will find that you can easily turn your left wrist and the putter to the left without moving your left arm — causing you to miss to your left. Now bring your left elbow out, so that it is pointing toward the hole or target. Get it way out there! (See the second picture.) With your elbow placed in this position, it is physically impossible for you to hit to the left unless your whole arm turns.

Now place your right hand on the club with the small finger of your right hand over the forefinger of your left hand. Your right thumb should also point straight down the top of the shaft. Now, by sliding out your left forefinger and placing it on top of the fingers of your right hand (as in the fourth picture) without disturbing the position of your hands, you will find it even more difficult to miss to the left.

Left hand remains over left thigh, thereby maintaining the natural loft on the putter blade.

Both hands are slightly to the right of the center of the left thigh.

Main pressure on the handle is supplied by the thumb and forefinger of the right hand.

Putter is securely locked in a grip that will give you firm-ness, yet extreme delicacy.

Hands are held at least one inch from end of putter handle.

Hands are taking up as little room as possible on the handle of the putter.

You now have your hands locked in a position that is mechanically perfect for accurate putting. Your grip on the putter should be light. The club should be held as lightly as though you were holding a small bird. You wouldn't let it sly away, but then you wouldn't crush it either.

This grip may feel very uncomfortable for a little while. But as you become accustomed to it you will be amazed at the accuracy and delicacy you can acquire in your putting. You are now ready for the basic putting stroke.

The Basic Putting Stroke

IN THE BASIC PUTTING stroke, the clubhead travels straight back about four inches and follows through approximately twelve inches as in the diagram in this chapter. The actual stroking is done with the arms, not with the wrists.

Why should you use the arm rather than the wrist? For this reason: The object of developing a good basic putting stroke is to create straight strokes of various lengths with the putter. Let's find out how we best can do this.

Try to draw a straight line with a pencil without moving your forearm, using only your fingers and wrist. You will find that you cannot draw a straight line more than a few inches long. Now try drawing a straight line, not using your wrist but only your arm. You will have no difficulty in drawing a straight line several feet long.

I repeat, the actual stroking is done not with the wrists, but with the arms. The right elbow stays close to the body throughout the stroke, brushing the right side gently as it goes back. If you start your putt back with your fingers or

12" FOLLOW-THROUGH

4"

PATH OF THE BASIC PUTTING STROKE

A diagram of this type can be laid out on the floor of your living room for practicing the basic putting stroke.

wrists, you may, under tension, close the clubface sharply as you stroke the ball, causing a pull to the left. Only when using your arms is it possible to keep the clubface square from the start to the finish of your putting stroke. *The point of energy comes from the right elbow.*

In short, take the club back with the right elbow. *The force that strokes the ball comes from the length of the stroke rather than from the strength applied.*

Practice your basic putting stroke by drawing a diagram similar to the one shown. Start at the point where the solid and dotted lines meet. Take a backswing to the end of the four-inch line and then follow through to the end of the twelve-inch line.

Practice this without a ball until you can follow the diagram quite easily. Then practice your basic putting stroke with a ball. Place the ball where the solid and dotted lines meet in the diagram. (If you put the diagram near a wall or any other solid object, the ball will bounce back to you without your having to retrieve it.) A few minutes of practice each evening for a few evenings will pay big dividends on the putting green.

When you feel that you have your basic putting stroke down pretty well, you are ready to start using a target. You can do this on your own living room rug. Let's use a really small target. Get a needle or a straight pin and stock it through a small piece of white paper, so that you can see it from a distance. Stick the pin, piercing through the paper, on your living room rug. Then mark off distances of one foot, two feet, three feet, and so on up to six feet. Mark off each foot with a coin of some similar object that will not mar your

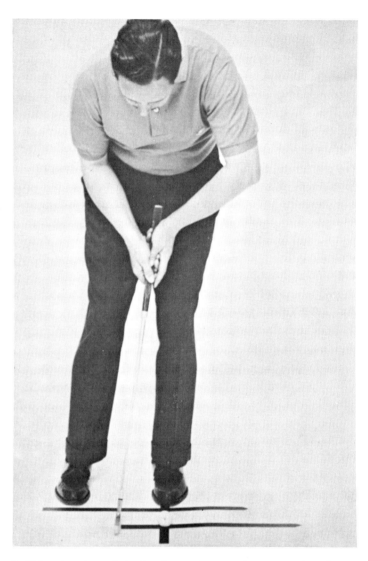

Full backswing of the basic putting stroke. Note the absence of wrist break.

In the follow-through of the basic putting stroke, the shaft is in the same relative position to the hands and arms as it was in the address. The clubhead must never be allowed to get ahead of the left wrist.

rug. Then start putting to the pin from the one-foot distance, hitting the pin six consecutive times.

Remember, you must hit the pin with the ball from the one-foot distance six consecutive times. If you get five hits and then a miss, you must start all over again. Only after you have hit the pin six consecutive times should you move back to the two-foot potision. You will find the pressure increasing as you hit the fifth and sixth putt.

After you have hit the pin six times in succession from the two-foot position, move back another foot until finally you are able to hit the pine six consecutive times from six feet. When you can do this, you are really putting!

The rewarding part of this exercise is that, once you have mastered it, it is only necessary for you to practice it once a month in order to maintain the patting skill you have acquired. There is no limit to the number of times you may hit the pin. Some of my pupils have worked this up to twelve times from each position.

Now, stop to think. You have been hitting a tiny pin, consistently, from one to six feet! The hole on the golf course is four and a quarter inches in diameter. When you are putting on the green, by comparison the hole will seem as large as a barrel.

By the way, when putting in long sessions, be sure you do not straighten up too fast, or you may pull a muscle in your back. Always get up slowly and you will not hurt yourself.

After you have developed a good degree of accuracy, you are ready to begin judging distances.

Judging Distance

LET'S FIND OUT, FOR certain, how far your ball will travel with the basic putting stroke. Go onto the practice putting green and stroke a few balls, using the basic putting stroke. Now measure the distance off in feet. You will notice that on a normal green the ball will travel approximately eight feet with the basic putting stroke (that is, with the four-inch backswing and the twelve-inch follow through). If the green is fast, the ball will travel approximately ten feet. A slow green will send the ball about six feet.

Before going out to play, test the practice green to find out how far your basic stroke will send the ball. The rest of the greens will usually be of approximately the same texture and speed. (Remember that the backswing of the basic putting stroke measures only four inches.)

Now, if your ball travels eight feet with the basic four-inch backstroke and you have a sixteen-foot putt, merely go back twice as far (eight inches). The follow-through remains the same. Similarly, as the length of the putt increases, increase the length of your backswing.

On the very long putts, play the ball just a little to the right of your left toe so as not to top it. Tee the ball on a line with the right side of your left foot.

Remember, the grass will not remain at the same texture from day to day. Therefore, it is wise to test the practice green before each round. If you haven't the time to go to the practice green, you can test the speed of the greens after you've played out the first hole, provided there is no one waiting

The basic putting circle is your target from six feet out. Once in the six-foot circle, you will be left with a putt of less than three feet.

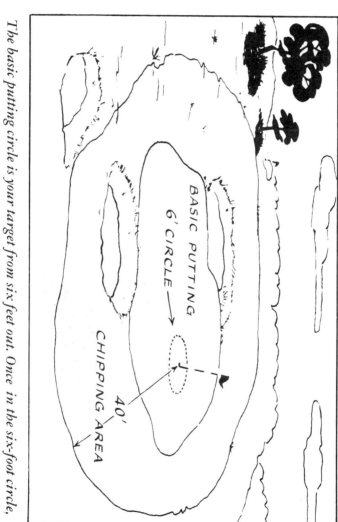

BASIC PUTTING
6' CIRCLE

CHIPPING AREA

40'

Body position at address remains the same in short as well as in long putts.

Note in the long putt the right elbow is still hugging the right side. The left wrist is still unbroken.

behind you to approach the green.

You are not allowed to test the green before playing out the hole. Needless to say, this would annoy your opponent very much, and, besides, the penalty is disqualification.

As you line up your putt, pace from your ball to the hole. (Each step or pace should be approximately three feet long.) Do it casually, so that your opponent will imagine that you are examining your line. If it is a very long putt, just pace halfway and really examine the path your ball must travel over, removing any pebble or foreign matter that is not growing on the green. You have now eliminated a lot of guess-work in your putting.

On the very long putts, visualize a six-foot circle around the hole and putt the ball into that circle, as close to its center as possible. Once in that circle, you will be left with a putt of under three feet. Then you can use your basic putting stroke. Be doing so, you will seldom need more than two putts on each green.

Reading the Greens

READING THE greens is a term that has confused quite a lot of golfers. It merely means being able to figure the line your ball must travel on its way to the hole.

To become a top-rank putter, having perfect mechanics, is a trememdous help. But you must know how to put to use your best putting techniques. It is like having a very fine rifle and expecting to hit your target without getting your sights in the proper alignment.

You actually start reading the green well before you get to

it. As you are walking up toward the green and you are still approximately a hundred and fifty yards away from it, take a look at it and study it, so that you can see in which direction the entire green is sloping. You can do this best while you are a little distance away from the green. Now, although the green may have many more slopes in it than you can see at a distance, you will have a great advantage while you are putting in knowing and remembering in which direction the entire green slopes.

If you are playing a course near the seashore, the greens will usually have a tendency to slope toward the ocean. If the course is in a mountainous area, the greens will usually slope away from the mountains. This will be so, even though your naked eye tells you otherwise.

After you have figured the general slope of the green from a distance, your next step, when your ball is on the green, is to figure the line from the ball to the hole. In doing this, your aim is to determine the texture of the grass along that intended line, the distance from the ball to the hole, and the amount of backswing and force needed to get the ball to the hole.

To get the best line from the ball to the hole, stand in back of the ball so that your master eye is doing the aligning. At times it is wise also to line up your putt from the hole to the ball. As you are lining up your putt, ask yourself this question: "If I were to roll a ball with my hand, which path should I take?" You will be amazed at how accurate that alignment will be.

After you have decided your line, then carefully inspect the grass along the line and pick up any specks of dirt that may be in the way. As you walk back from the hole to the ball casually, to give you some idea of how much backswing to take. Do not be afraid to take all your time surveying your putt — a missed putt is a stroke lost for good.

I repeat, on the very long putts, your aim is to make the ball stop in the center of that imaginary six-foot circle around the hole, so as to leave yourself a very short putt in case of a miss. At times, there may be a double roll in the line toward the hole. It is advisable to play the roll closest to the hole. A fast-traveling ball will not be affected so much by a slope as will a slow-traveling ball.

The area of the six-foot basic putting circle is where you must be most observant — to the point of examining the direction in which the blades of grass are growing — for they will also affect the roll of the ball. A ball will always break in the direction that the blades of grass are growing. If you have a short, straight putt, you must decide whether to hit the ball a little more firmly or to stroke it gently and allow for the slight break you will get from the direction of the grain, grass, or nap of the green.

The best way to stroke a short putt is to stroke it firmly. A ball that is stroked firmly will hold its line, while a ball that is stroked very softly is left at the mercy of the elements.

Start keeping track of the number of putts you are taking for the eighteen holes; and, after a few rounds of golf, you will be amazed at the number of strokes you are saving. With this system of putting, you will be surprised at how well you will be able to cope with any situation that arises on the green.

The Chip Shot

THE CHIP SHOT IS one of the most important shots in golf. You can hit your drive not quite right, miss the green with your second shot, chip up to the pin for one putt, and still get your par.

The chip shot is the great equalizer in golf. Miss your chip shot and what would have been a par for the hole turns out to be a bogey, or possibly a double bogey. The chip shot is the shot that makes up the difference when a shorter hitter gets up against a long hitter. The short hitter must then depend on his chip shot to get his par, because he lacks the length to reach the long par four holes with his second shot. Whenever the green is missed, it depends upon the chip shot to make par possible.

The chip shot requires the same delicacy and touch that is so necessary in putting. The stroke you use for a long putt is the stroke that you should use for a chip shot. A good putter is usually a good chipper.

Use the same grip for chipping that you are using for putting, with both thumbs on top of the shaft so that the palms of each hand face each other. The reason for this is that the position of the palms affects the two large bones in the forearm called the ulna and the radius bones. When the palms are faced downward, these two bones cross each other, giving the golfer less delicacy in his touch. When the ulna and radius bones are not crossed, there is a greater sensitivity in the hands.

In chipping we need all the touch and feel of which we are

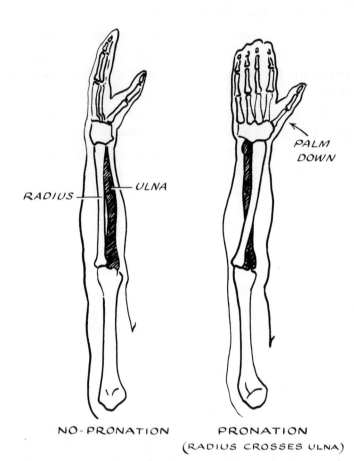

RADIUS — ULNA

PALM DOWN

NO-PRONATION

PRONATION
(RADIUS CROSSES ULNA)

Sketch showing effect on the bones of the forearm when the hand is turned or pronated. The greatest sensitivity of the fingers is attained when the ulna and radius bones are not crossed.

capable. The arms and hands do all the work — that is why the position of the hands is so vital.

The stance is square as it is in the putt, with the feet just a little farther apart. The body weight is mostly on the left foot and toward the heels. Body movement in a chip shot is at a minimum.

The only difference between a long putt and a chip shot is the choice of club and the longer backswing and follow-through. The maximum backswing for a chip shot is reached when your club shaft is horizontal to the ground, the follow-through being equal.

The target for the chip shot is the same as in putting. You chip for the imaginary circle, six feet in diameter, around the hole. Once in that circle, you are left with a basic putt of less than three feet, making it quite possible to get down in one putt. You will even be surprised to see quite a few chip shots go into the cup.

I know you are quite anxious to find out which club to use in chipping; so let's go down to the practice green, taking your 7-, 8-, and 9-irons with you. Now, while you are on the apron of the green, take your 9-iron and a few practice balls and chip a few balls onto the green, using the putting stroke. Remember to play the ball just a little to the right of the left toe, in line with the right side of your left foot.

Take a few full chip shots with your 9-iron. Also remember that, in a full chip shot, the clubhead goes back about waist high up to the point where the shaft of your club is level or horizontal to the ground. The follow-through will be equally as long. The energy that strokes the ball comes from the size of the circle rather than from the force supplied.

229

After you have taken about a dozen full chip shots, you will notice that the balls are bunched at approximately the same distance away from where you were chipping. Now start pacing off from where you were chipping to the center of the group of balls. You will find that the average distance that the ball traveled was approximately forty paces. Now, if a full chip with a 9-iron travels forty paces, a half chip shot will travel half that distance: twenty paces. If, in a full chip shot, the clubhead goes back to the point where the shaft of the club is horizontal to the ground, in a half chip shot the clubhead will go back half the distance of a full chip shot, halfway between the horizontal point and the ground. A quarter chip shot, in turn, will go back only half the distance of a half chip shot. And so, if a full chip shot with a 9-iron will send the ball approximately forty paces or forty yards and a half chip shot, also with the 9-iron, will send the ball about twenty paces or twenty yards, then a quarter chip shot will send the ball about ten paces, and so forth.

A full chip shot with an 8-iron will travel about five paces more than with a 9-iron: approximately forty-five paces. A full chip shot with a 7-iron will send the ball still another five paces: approxiomately fifty paces.

You key club in chipping is your 9-iron. Under normal conditions, it should be used for anything up to forty paces, although almost any iron can be used successfully in chipping. The great advantage in chipping with your 9-iron is that the ball can be stroked more firmly. Therefore, it will cover most of the distance in the air and will not be influenced by a bad bounce off the apron of the green.

The Chip Shot: *The stance is the same as in the putt, except that the ball is played just off the right side of the left foot. This brings your ball to the bottom of the stroking arc, thereby eliminating topping.*

The Quarter Chip Shot: *Used for short distances.*

The Half Chip Shot: *Note left wrist beginning to straighten out slightly.*

The Full Chip Shot: *Note right wrist is almost straight. There is a minimum of body movement. The knees are still facing straight ahead. Body weight is still on left.*

Follow-through for the short chip shot. The clubhead must not be permitted to get ahead of the left wrist. Left elbow still points out, but is raised.

Follow-through for full chip shot. Again, clubhead should not be permitted to get ahead of the left wrist.

237

Strive to make your ball land on the green on its first bounce. With a lofted club like the 9-iron, you can do this without fear of running too far past the hole. You can chip right for the pin; for a 9-iron will give the ball a slight degree of backspin. You will also find this especially useful when going over a trap or a bunker.

When more loft and backspin are needed, a chip with your wedge will make the ball stop even more quickly. At times, when the lie is good and the trap shallow, a chip out of the trap with your 9-iron will produce amazing results.

You have now eliminated quite a lot of guesswork in your putting and chipping. Just a little practice will enable you to get down in two from any distance up to fifty yards. A little time spent in practicing this putting and chipping method will be rewarded by less wastage of strokes and lower scores.

Bi-monthly Practice Routine

THE FOLLOWING pages describe a rather specific routine to improve the putting and chipping techniques you have learned in this book. By devoting one morning of extensive practice to these "exercises" you will exhibit marked improvement in your game for approximately two months. Spend approximately four hours on your putting and chipping drills to insure satisfactory results.

Putting

LET'S BEGIN with putting practice. Remember to incorporate the suggestions that I have offered. And, above all, try to make these incorporations unconscious reactions. Try to get to the point where you can do them without thinking about them — do them as if you've been doing them all your life.

On a practice putting green, draw an imaginary circle around the cup, at a radius of one foot from the cup. Using this one-foot putt as the starting point, place balls at various points around the circle and practice sinking them until you can sink six consecutive putts from this distance.

Now expand your imaginary circle until it has a two-foot radius. Again, with the balls placed around the circumference of the circle, practice putting until you sink six consecutively from the two-foot mark.

Continue to expand your circle to three feet, four, five, and finally six feet. Remember, you must sink six balls consecutively from each distance before going on to the next distance. You are only cheating yourself if you move farther out without sinking all the balls.

Now you are ready to attempt longer putts.

Make a three-foot jump in the radius of your imaginary circle to nine feet and attempt several putts (about fifteen or twenty) from this distance. Your object from the longer distances will be to putt as close to the cup as possible, not to sink any consecutve number. After you have become fairly proficient from nine feet, move to twelve feet, then fifteen, and finally eighteen — in each case, attempting to get as close as possible.

This simple drill, with the aids offered in other parts of the book, will enable you to cut many putting strokes off your total score. You will be amazed at how your score will drop.

Chipping

LET'S CONCENTRATE on your chip shot. Again, I urge you to incorporate all the techniques and pointers you've learned earlier in this book. If you learn these pointers until they become habits, chipping will come very easily.

Begin your chip shot drill about three yards from the pin. With your 9-iron, chip at least two dozen balls. Continue chipping until you are able to place all the balls withing a one-putt area of the pin.

Now move out another three yards. You are now six yards out. Still using your 9-iron, practice chipping until you can place two dozen balls within a one-putt area of the pin. This one-putt area is determined by your ability to sink putts consistently from a particular distance.

Continue to move out at three-yard intervals, chipping to the one-putt area with your 9-iron. When you have reached your maximum chipping distance with the 9-iron, switch to the 8-iron, and continue with the same idea in mind — to get within a one-putt area of the pin.

Practice chipping with the 8-iron by moving out at three-yard intervals until you have reached a maximum distance. Then, change to your 7-iron, always attempting to place each ball within a one-putt distance of the pin. Once more, move out until you have reached the maximum distance for the 7-iron.

Consistency is what you should strive for in all golf drills, and in your every movement on the links. Keeping this in mind, along with the learning process in which you practice until your movememts become unconscious reactions, you can clip many strokes off your score and enjoy your game more and more with each new round.

BOOK III

THE FINESSE SHOTS OF GOLF

The Finesse' Shots of Golf

Playing Position

IN PLAYING POSITION on the golf course, do so right from the first tee. Don't figure you will start warming up as you go along. You should start playing as though the first hole is the last hole and the most important hole of your match, and, you must get a birdie to win.

In fact you should start thinking and planning your round even before you get to the first tee. But, if you have not had a chance to have played the course, start planning your strategy from the moment you start preparing to tee up your ball. Now as you are on the tee looking down the fairway, in your imagination visualize a highway running right down the middle of the fairway. Then, visualize four lanes with four vehicles traveling side by side on the imaginary road. There is usually enough room on the average fairway for more than four cars to fit side by side, so there is plenty of room for your tiny golf ball to fit on the fairway.

The Fairway Road

NOW, in your imagination put a white line right down the middle of your fairway road. Figure out on which side of this white line the most trouble lies. When you have done that, play across the center line to the other side of the fairway road. Very rarely should you play for the center of the fairway. Always play for either the left side or the right side. If the conditions are normal and there is not too much trouble on either side of the fairway, then ask yourself this question, "From which side of the fairway would it be easier to land on the green?"

So, on the tee of each hole use these three keys:

(1)   Mentally dissect your fairway in half by drawing an imaginary line right up the middle.

(2)   On which side of the fairway does the greater danger lie?

(3)   From which side of the fairway is it easier to shoot to the green?

Green Strategy

AFTER YOU HAVE HIT your tee shot and are now in range of the green, mentally cut your green in half right down the middle, and then dissect it horizontally in half again making four quarters. Now, which is the easiest quarter to hit? Which is the quarter the flag is resting in?

Is it wisest to shoot for the safest part of the green or go for the section in which the flag is resting? Use your own judgment. If you feel confident that you can hit the section where the flag is resting, by all means go for it. Do not be timid. But, for the players that are ot quite as skillful as the experts, go for the safest part of the green.

If it is the first time you are playing a course, play position on each hole as has been suggested. But for the golfers who play the same course repeatedly, at some time make a sketch of each hole. Dissect the fairway green of each hole, and then, put a dot on the fairway and another on the green to indicate where to play positions on each particular fairway and green. Keep in mind that when it does not matter from which side of the fairway you approach the green and when there is little or no trouble on either side of the fairway, it is advisable for a right-handed player to tee up on the left side of the teeing area and hit to the right side of the imaginary fairway road and vice versa for the left-handed player.

This teeing position will help keep your stroke on the correct inside out path. In all instances, never just swing aimlessly. Pick a spot and hope to get as close to the spot as possible. Don't worry if you hit the ball off the line, there is no golfer in the world accurate enough to hit the ball exactly where he would like it to go. If there were, the scores would be in the fifties. The top golfers pick a spot to shoot for on the fairway or on the green and then, shoot for the spot and accept the results whether good or bad like confirmed fatalists. The development of this attitude toward accuracy is the one barrier that ordinary players must cross to become top golfers.

Low Ball Against Wind

NOW that you've mapped out your course, start planning individual shots. Consider each shot before you play it. On these pages are two typical problem shots, and suggestion on how to hit them. When playing against the wind, tilt the tee forward into the wind and also play the ball farther back toward the middle. In this way, the ball will have a lower trajectory, for less wind resistance. Do not hit harder, in fact swing easier.

High Ball With Wind

WHEN playing with the wind, tilt the tee backwards as illustrated and play the ball slightly forward so as to give the ball a higher trajectory thereby allowing the wind to help

243

give you greater distance. Do not hit harder, in fact, swing slower, about the same strength as hitting into the wind.

Ball Compression

FEW GOLFERS realize the importance of ball compression. To see how compression can affect the ball, take a golf ball and drop it from shoulder height on a wooden surface. It would take great effort to get maximum bounce from a golf ball on a wooden surface. However, if you were to drop a golf ball on a concrete surface you would find it bounces much higher. The ordinary wooden surface does not give enough resistance to dent the ball and compress it full; the harder concrete surface does.

Keep in mind then that your swing must be fast and powerful enough to dent and decompress a high compression golf ball. If you cannot swing that fast, try a ball with less compression. To determine which type of ball to use, first determine the average length of your drive. If your drives are under 220 yards then high compression balls are not for you. But if your average drives are above 220 yards you should use the highest compression golf ball.

Experiment with different brands and compressions and ask the advice of your club pro to help you select the ball best suited for your swing.

Another point to keep in mind when selecting a ball is that temperature has an effect on compression and elasticity of the ball. Cool rubber is not as elastic as warm rubber, and so in colder weather you should use a ball of lower compression. On a very hot day, switch to a ball with higher compression.

Vital Stages of Swing

NOW FOR THE PAY-OFF of all the planning that has appeared on the pages before this. You are ready to drive, and now comes some of the most vital sections in the swing.

The backswing ● At the top of the backswing, your wrists are fully cocked (don't worry about the length of the backswing, the position of the club shaft is regulated by the flexibility of your wrists). The height of the left arm should be between your right ear and right shoulder. Your shoulders are turned fully and your body is in a position to deliver a full, powerful blow through the ball and into the followthrough.

Start of the downswing ● It is advisable to start the downswing with the pull of only the left arm. In doing so you should feel as though your body is being kept out of the shot. In actuality the body will move first — the trick is to try and hold it back. Only when you become an expert golfer should you consciously start the downswing with a movement of the left hip.

Contact point ● This is the climax of your swing, what happens now is the result of what you have done before. If you consciously try to arrive at an exact contact position, you will not be able to do so. At this instant, it all should happen by itself, your mind should be blank. If you hesitate even to check if you are correct at contact point, a missed shot will surely follow. Contact point is the instant of full release and should happen naturally.

Follow-through ● The follow-through is a result of great speed through the elimination of all restrictions in the swing. The parts of the body that can be most detrimental to a full follow-through are the head and the right heel. If you try to keep your head down throughout the swing you will restrict the follow-through. If you don't come up on your right toe, you will also restrict the follow-through. The most vital actions of the full follow-through are the turning of the head after contact point, and the coming up on your right toe at the finish. These two actions are a **must** for great club head speed and are also helpful in preventing back and spine injury to the less flexible golfer.

The Downhill Lie

IN THIS SHOT, open your stance slightly and play the ball off your right heel. The right knee should be bent more than normal and more than the left knee. Use a more lofted club than the shot calls for. The ball will fade slightly so allow for that as well.

A simple rule to remember in both uphill and downhill lies is to always play the ball closer to the **higher** foot.

The Uphill Lie

IN HITTING an uphill lie, keep the left knee bent a little more than normal in an effort to keep your back level. The ball will then have a tendency to hook so allow for this in setting your swing. In selecting a club, use one club stronger than you would normally use. The uphill lie tends to cause a hook.

Ball Above

WHEN BALL is above level of your feet, stand taller from the waist up, shorten grip and play the ball as though it were on a normal lie. A stronger club may be used as shortening of the hold will take away some power.

Ball Below

WHEN BALL is below, bend slightly more from the waist and stretch down more with the arms. The ball will tend to go further than usual so allow for this, and swing same as in normal lie.

Intentional Hook

THERE ARE TIMES when it is necessary to play a hook shot, and of course those are just the times that the struggling golfer will hit the straight ball. Thus it is helpful to know how to play an intentional hook and to use this shot as part of your arsenal of strategic weapons.

In placing an intentional hook, turn both hands more to the right than usual and close your stance by stepping forward slightly with your left foot. Aim more toward the right to allow for the right-to-left curve of the ball.

Intentional Slice

MOST GOLFERS try to avoid the slice as they would a plague. But here again, there are occasions when a slice is a valuable means of saving one or two strokes, so it is helpful to know how to hit one when you need it.

In the intentional slice, turn both hands toward the left and step back slightly with the left foot. This will cause you to cut the ball from the outside of the line of flight. Use a stronger club, as a fade will take some of the length from your shot.

Pitch Shot

THERE ARE TIMES when a full shot will get your ball to travel too far. It is necessary to know when to diminish your power, and how to do it.

In making a pitch shot, tee the ball further back toward the right heel and place your right foot at a perfect right angle to the line of flight left toe out. This placement of the right foot will cause a restriction in your backswing, thus giving you a more controlled shot with a lower trajectory.

The Cut Shot

THE CUT SHOT is executed from the same stance as the pitch shot. Right foot straight, left toe out. The club face is more open than usual and the swing is in the outside-in path. The ball and the turf must be hit at the same time as this shot is actually a blast from the turf. Don't baby the shot, hit it firmly.

The Trap Shot

OF COURSE the best way to get out of a trap is not to get into one, but at times this is difficult to avoid. Every good golfer must know what to do once he's in a trap.

To get out of a trap the easiest way is to blast out. In blasting out of the trap, first make sure that your feet are sunk below the level of the ball. Your body should be bent a little more than usual as shown in the sketch. The blade in a normal trap shot must be slightly opened. Hit the sand the same distance in back of the ball as the diameter of the ball. In blasting out when the ball is buried, don't open the club face — close it.

Try to cultivate an even, moderate tempo in your trap shots.

The Chip Shot

THE CHIP SHOT is a long putt. The grip is the same as that for putting. Holding the club in this manner gives you great control and exceptional feel. As in putting, the stroking is done with the right hand and arm in control. The feet are parallel and knees bent; the weight is on the left foot and slightly back toward the heels.

In the follow-through of the chip shot, the shaft should be in the same relation to the left hand as at the start of the swing. Do not allow the club head to get ahead of your left hand. Use the 8-iron as the key club for chipping. If more length is needed, use a stronger club. If less length is needed, use a 9-iron.